MW01168849

For Joanna, David
and family,

With warmest regards,

Harvey

Feb. 28, 2004

YOUR FAMILY
IS GOOD FOR YOU

HARVEY WHITE, M.D.

YOUR FAMILY
IS GOOD FOR YOU

RANDOM HOUSE
NEW YORK

Copyright © 1978 by Harvey White, M.D.

All rights reserved under International and Pan-
American Copyright Conventions. Published in the
United States by Random House, Inc., New York, and
simultaneously in Canada by Random House of
Canada Limited, Toronto.

Library of Congress Cataloging in Publication Data
White, Harvey, 1938-
Your family is good for you.
1. Family psychotherapy. 2. Family. I. Title
RC488.5.W49   362.8'2   77-90307
ISBN 0-394-40925-6

Manufactured in the United States of America
2 4 6 8 9 7 5 3
First Edition

To the memory of my brother Floyd

When the father is in truth a father, and the son a son, when the elder brother is an elder brother, and the younger brother a younger brother, a husband a husband and a wife a wife, then the house is on the right way. When the house is set in order, the world is set in order, the world is established on a firm course. **I CHING**

ACKNOWLEDGMENTS

INITIAL ENCOURAGEMENT for this book came from Alan Rinzler whose friendship ever since our undergraduate days has been so important to me. His guidance and energy throughout the project were crucial, especially when the material seemed to overwhelm the book, and me with it.

I am indebted to my editor, Toni Morrison, whose vision and insight helped keep my own sense of discovery alive.

I owe a primary debt to Dr. George Gero for, among other things, my education in psychoanalysis and without whom this book would never have been written.

I am grateful to the members of my own family for their love, tolerance, encouragement, and honest criticism. It was especially gratifying to meet with members of my extended family, in Atlanta and Miami, while working on this book.

I thank my three research assistants, Henny Drucker, Peter Zimmermann, and my cousin Ed Gordon who helped with much of the material. I would also like to mention the most important teacher early in my life, Jennie Ward Bogert, who nurtured my sensibility and who would have been happy to know of this effort.

And much appreciation, of course, goes to all my patients who taught me so much: those on the Indian reservation in North Dakota where (when I was seventeen years old) I was first called "Doc," those in New Jersey where I practiced general medicine, and those in New York where I practice and teach family psychiatry. I am especially grateful to those who said:

"Someone ought to write a book about this."

CONTENTS

INTRODUCTION

EARLY IN MY CAREER as a physician I came to realize that a deep understanding of oneself through one's family could be the key to healing,
growth, and fulfillment. Nearly all of us have grown up in a family of
one sort or another. In dealing with people with physical or emotional
problems—whether in their homes, in my office, or in emergency
rooms—I discovered that the family out of which the individual
emerged was always like the sea, the milieu that could explain and
restore him. When thinking about someone's problems, I almost automatically referred to the family around him. Also, the more contact I
had with different kinds of people, the more I came to understand that
the family has grown beyond the old myth of the nuclear family. There
are many kinds of families: flexibly extended nuclear ones, one-parent,
and "blended" families. Although the family is evolving as an institution, statistics confirm my belief that the family is here to stay. It remains everyone's best hope for safe passage on the life course.

IN RECENT YEARS it has become fashionable to criticize the family and to
condemn it as an outmoded institution responsible for our individual
inhibitions, emotional sufferings, and for various "ills" of our society.
Yet most of those who blame the family grew up in one, and the great
majority of people today, in every society, still grow up in a family of
some sort. Most of us still learn to experience love, trust, anger, and excitement for the first time in a family, and it is through dealing with
these emotions that we become whole human beings, able to address
ourselves to those around us in a society that changes day by day, minute by minute, and challenges our very existence.

Among the critics of the family are those who say the family is the
primary mechanism of a reactionary society, self-perpetuated by its crea-

tion of reactionary individuals. To change our society the family must be eliminated. There is no doubt that as the crucible for emotional and social development, the family molds the individual for society, bringing the complex network of society's value systems, purposes, culture, and style to bear on each person. Our political views and expectations are determined, to an extent, by how much responsibility we feel toward the needs of others, and this feeling, in turn, is a reflection of how we work through conflicts at certain earlier stages in development—conflicts, for instance, over dependency and aggression. For the most part, however, the family only provides the mechanism whereby values and cultural traditions are passed on to the individual. It reflects rather than creates those values.

Moreover, if it is a reshaping rather than the destruction of society that we seek, an understanding of the pathways by which social forces affect the individual can provide us with the mechanism for desirable change. Through understanding the way in which wars, migrations, epidemics, economic depression, and affluence affect us emotionally (they are felt by us insofar as they cause separations, bereavements, pervasive emotional attitudes, and conflicts in important family figures), we can not only alleviate individual emotional suffering, but as a society we can survive and endure. Through seeing how outside forces influence our daily concerns and our family value systems, and through learning how all these influences challenge and change the family's coping ability (affecting not only roles and values but the family's sense of time, space, and style of communication), we can adapt and even control the forces that threaten to destroy us.

One of our problems as a society is that we continue to view current issues in terms of yesterday's fears and adaptations. Through understanding the mechanism by which social forces exist in a constant equilibrium with emotions in every individual and are carried on into the future, we can truly know the past, its challenges, and how they were met by modes of adaptation appropriate for those times. Our families can drag us down, forcing us, unaware, to dedicate our lives to men, women, and issues of the past. We can spend our lives endlessly working through feelings that only serve to limit and imprison us, feelings that first arose in our parents and grandparents in response to events and accidents of their time; feelings that were imprinted on family structures and are memorialized by our lives today. By understanding our families, by learning how to work and grow within them, we can realize our potential as individuals.

Every event that affects us is mediated through the family. In a secure family situation we are protected, able to survive experiences that would otherwise crush us, whether they are personal tragedies, social upheavals, or even natural disasters. Thus protected, we are finally liberated, able to work toward our own fulfillment, to pass freely in and out of the family for work and play, and ultimately to turn our attention toward building a secure world for others.

Another category of anti-family thinking is concerned with the apparent crumbling of the family as a viable institution. The fact that one out of two marriages ends in separation or divorce, the growing number of single-parent families, the increased dissatisfaction voiced by married people, and the emotional problems shown by their children all affect the image of the family and force us to ask questions. Is the family appropriate as the framework for our basic set of permanent relationships? What can we expect from our families? Why are families falling apart, why can't we be happier, and how can we work toward more adaptive, more satisfying family lives? These questions can be answered only in part by sociological studies of the family and its evolution; they can be answered more fully by an understanding of our biological and emotional needs and how they are met by families, and by seeing what styles and tendencies our families are heir to.

THE FAMILY can be defined as a small group of individuals with intense one-to-one relationships or bonds in which the welfare of one affects all. It is the framework best equipped to handle individuals of more than one generation, individuals of different age levels and different needs from those around them. In the most obvious way, for instance, the physical and emotional needs of infants differ from those of adults. The family is built, therefore, to contain divergence and allows the individual to grow and to change. When it fulfills its functions successfully it becomes the smallest unit of a larger group, a society. This family form of living for survival, growth, development, and procreation exists throughout the world, goes back through centuries of recorded civilization, and is even found among primates. It is the unit that has evolved to meet the physical and emotional needs of its members. These needs include the need to be loved and valued, and to learn to love, value, and trust others; the need to be controlled and to learn to control oneself; the need to accept the pleasure and potential of one's identity as a person, as a male or female, and finally to turn to people outside the family for gratification of these needs in a stable way. All of these early needs are met and worked through in an intense one-to-one caring relationship, sometimes with one parent or parental figure, sometimes with the other, through a complex series of psychological mechanisms that allows one to become whole as a person and to grow away from the primary family. The family varies at different places and in different times, and reflects changing individual needs and changing societies. The time frame with which the family adapts, however, is built into the biology of its individuals. This fixed time schedule for physical and emotional development, as contrasted with a fluid world of rapidly changing institutions, expanded opportunities, easy disorganization, and chaotic variability makes for some of the problems that burden the family today.

I have discovered, however, that the main problem individuals have with their family lives does not have to do with the inadequacy of the family as an institution. Family satisfaction depends on the ability to transfer meaningful and satisfying attachments from primary families of origin to new families of our own making.

The problem is threefold:

1. Feelings like anger, fear, or desire that come from unresolved conflicts and attachments toward our parents, whoever and wherever they are, in our adult lives, prevent us from seeing and experiencing others in a realistic and whole way.

2. Even if we are released from the constraints of earlier relationships, it takes courage, work, and life experience to understand ourselves, to know our feelings, to tolerate, express, and sometimes to limit our emotions toward intimates.

3. Just as we often do not know ourselves, we do not know our families. We frequently fail to understand how they evolved from two different families of origin, what they do for each family member, and how we can work on them. We mindlessly force, bend and break family structures to meet our own needs, each of us unaware of the pattern of the whole.

In this book I have at times combined details of a number of cases or exaggerated features of family types. I have done this to show how families operate as systems, how they affect each individual, how we are all products of our families and carry our families around with us, and finally, how we can grow beyond our limited view of ourselves and our possibilities. It has been my experience, from working as a therapist with families and from hearing about others who were coming to terms with their families by themselves, that with work, guidance, and patience an understanding of our past and present interpersonal milieu is the best approach to solving problems and finding a transcendent meaning for our lives. It is my hope that this book will help you analyze and understand yourself and your family in a new way, and that you will be able to exercise this understanding to realize your own potential for satisfaction and to help those around you realize theirs.

YOUR FAMILY
IS GOOD FOR YOU

1

THE K. FAMILY: HOW FAMILIES WORK

Billy k. junior had been in the hospital for a week because of a serious suicide attempt. After two years of depression, guilt, fights with his parents, heavy drinking, and weekend drug use, he threw in the towel, took all the barbiturates in the family medicine cabinet and drove to a deserted parking lot. He was found quite by accident by an auxiliary policeman.

A week after being in the hospital he and his psychiatrist decided to ask his family to come in and talk about what had happened and what was happening right then at home.

The family was sitting in a circle when the two therapists, a psychiatrist and a social worker, came in. Mother and daughter Ginny were comfortable in one corner, backs to the wall, with a good view of the room. Father and Jimmy, the youngest, were across from Mother. Billy Junior, Susan, and Kathy formed the rest of the semicircle, leaving chairs between Mother and themselves for the therapists. Father pulled his chair forward, almost reaching toward Mother, closing off the circle. The family members were comfortable, joked with one another, and seemed ready to "take on" the therapists, to like them and be liked by them. Considering the number of problems and their seriousness, it came almost as a surprise that it was pleasant and comfortable to be with this family. Billy Junior had been seriously suicidal. Bill Senior had a twenty-year history of heavy drinking, resulting finally in liver damage. Mother had been having serious depressions for the last few years and Jimmy had problems at school.

The session had no beginning. After they introduced themselves the therapists joined in as the family members chatted about the therapists' office, about shrinks, about Bob Newhart, and various other topics. Mother was pleasant; she talked infrequently, but when she did, everybody listened. Everybody watched her for cues. Father fought hard to be heard. There was lots of noise and a few of the children seemed nervous. Mother seemed to rule the roost, and the girls were more relaxed than the boys. The teenagers—Ginny, Billy, Susie, and Kathy—were attractive and graceful, comfortable with their bodies.

After ten minutes one of the therapists pulled the session together.

"What's happening in the family now? Where are you at?"

Jimmy was the first to speak. "There is too much fighting all the time."

Kathy and Susie disagreed. "Not everybody." They looked at their mother.

"Only certain people are fighting all the time. The two of them are always fighting."

Kathy pointed to Mother and Father, who were sitting opposite each other, separated by the diameter of the circle.

Father seemed annoyed, but he smiled. "We argue, but not all the time. We have some good days."

Mother came right to the point. "It's your drinking, Bill. When he's drunk he gets very abusive to me and the children and I'm just not going to stand for it anymore."

Now he let his anger show. "Everything is my drinking. You're Miss Innocent, I suppose. When did I get drunk, when was I abusive?"

After a few minutes a therapist cut this off: "What else goes on in the family?"

Mother began speaking. "Everything is just too much. The kids need me, he needs me, I don't have any time to myself. I go to work eight o'clock in the morning. Between his job and my job we can hardly make ends meet. He won't go anywhere with me. I like to go out. I get fidgety just sitting home. I have trouble sleeping."

Mother was overwhelmed and probably depressed.

The family members assumed they were in this office because there was too much arguing at home, because they did not have enough control. For the children, coming to the therapist was like coming to the principal's office.

They were finished warming up, and the session began in earnest. Each blamed one or two others for wrong-doing, and the chief wrong-doing was selfishness, demandingness, and anger. There were arguments over emotional "supplies" from Mother.

Susan and Kathy: "They [the boys] get anything they want from you. You can't say no."

Jimmy: "I do not."

Kathy: "He can make his own breakfast. He's ten years old."

Bill Senior: "They all get away with murder and you let them. Children their age should be helping you."

A therapeutic rule of thumb is to think about what the family members do not talk about. If the family came in talking about Billy Junior's accidents and overdose, a therapist would think about the conflicts between the others. Now that they were blaming each other for anger, weakness, and selfishness, the therapists thought about Billy. Thinking was one thing, talking was another. Everyone shouted and no one listened in this family.

Therapist: "I'd like to . . . hold it a minute, Susie . . . could I say . . . can I ask? . . ."

He knew it would be useless to try to get through. But he wanted to know what it would be like, the futility of trying to get a word in edgewise, of not really being heard no matter how hard he tried. The therapists looked at each other, unnoticed by the family. One of them stood up, looked around the room and began asking different family members to move their chairs. The conversation stopped abruptly.

Jimmy smiled and whispered to his father: "That's not polite."

"Polite?" asked the therapist. "How do you mean? I don't want to be impolite, but how should I signal when I want to say something?"

"Raise your hand," said Susan.

The therapist looked at Susan for a few moments. Everybody in the family waited for his reply. His silence had silenced them. It was different from the rest of the session.

Therapist: "Mrs. K., can I call you Jean? . . . Can I ask you to move your chair next to your husband? Ginny, could you move over here?"

The therapist divided up the family into two subgroups, parents and children. Mother was uncomfortable but smiling.

Mother: "I don't think I like this." She smiled. "I don't want this."

Father was embarrassed. "We do fight a lot." Now he was ready to confess just to avoid the emotion everyone was beginning to feel.

Therapist: "Can I make a suggestion? Only one person talk at a time. I think the problem sometimes is listening to each other, hearing each other. When you hear something, don't talk. Think about it for a moment. Now, what can we accomplish here today? What are you really worried about? I think I've heard enough about your complaints. What, if anything, can we do here today?"

Father: "We're here because of Billy. His pills, his drinking, and driving."

Mother continued: "Can we say anything? I mean . . . we all know . . . I don't want to hurt anybody's feelings, but it's the second time he tried this. I don't know . . ."

She began to cry. "Why would he want to commit suicide?"

She shook as she cried, she moaned almost as if she were having labor pains. The children were in tears. Susan moved away from Billy Junior in anger. Billy Senior tried to console his wife.

She pushed him away. "If he had any kind of a father in the first place, he wouldn't be in this mess. Don't touch me."

Her husband stood up in a rage. "That's all you can do is blame me. It's all my fault, everything. You go save him."

He was screaming at his wife. The social worker went to Jean and held her. She first tried lamely to push her away and then cried in her arms. Ginny, Susan, and Kathy were fidgety at first, angry at the men, their father, Billy Junior, and they even looked angrily at Jimmy. After a while they settled down and shared their mother's pain.

Bill Senior interrupted. "You're feeling sorry for yourself." He could not tolerate his wife's crying. (When she went into her own feelings he felt deserted.) After a few minutes the social worker took Bill Senior's arm so that he and the therapist were holding his wife. Gradually he replaced the woman therapist. The loud, busy family suddenly became a tribal séance with Mother sobbing in her husband's arms. This went on for a full five minutes. Jean eventually stopped crying. The male therapist moved over to Billy Junior and asked what he had been feeling. They had had a session the previous day in preparation for the family meeting.

Billy Junior: "I wanted to get up and leave, really felt an urge to run. I started blaming myself and just as I thought how ridiculous it was to feel guilty, Susie looked at me and Ginny looked at me and even my father, they were all looking at me. As if it was all my fault. It's like a conspiracy. It all fits. It hurt, but I can handle it."

Therapist, to the other children: "It's hard, isn't it? There's so much pain in this family. You run away from it. You think it will kill somebody . . . your mother . . . if it comes out in the open. It won't kill her, tears never killed anyone."

Bill Senior was still holding his wife. The therapist touched his shoulder.

Therapist: "She can't ask you for help or thank you, but you did real well. Mom, how long have you had this kind of pain?"

Mother: "For years."

Therapist: "How many years?"

Mother: "Two or three. Two years ago I remember there were a couple of months which were awful. Grandma died in October . . . What does any of this have to do with Billy?"

Therapist: "Your grandmother?"

Mother: "That was hard. Everything was happening at once. She brought me up, my brothers and sister. I was the baby. We were very close. My mother died when we were young and my father left us with her parents on the farm. He went up to Chicago. He visited us now and then at first, but later we only saw him once in a while. We'd get Christmas presents from him. He died ten years ago, he drank himself to death. My grandparents raised us. Grandpa was very strict. He bossed everyone around. I was the baby and I was named after my mother's sister. My grandmother and I were so close."

She began crying again. "It was hard . . . even when I got married I was depressed. Bill was drinking, he'd come home drunk, sometimes he hit me; a couple of times I packed up the kids and went back home. She'd send me back, though." The tears came again.

Therapist: "How did she die?"

Mother: "She was old, she had heart trouble. She was living with us the last few years of her life. We stayed with her around the clock, my sister and I, and at the end she wanted my uncles, her sons. Uncle Roy. That hurt. She couldn't help herself, I guess, but after all we loved her and after all we did, she wanted them. It was like that all my life. Whatever my brothers did they made a fuss over. It's like we didn't count." She cried again.

When she stopped the therapist said, "There is a lot of pain that you still have. Everyone in the family tries to distract you, but it's better if you feel it."

Jean's life history of problem after problem began with the death of her mother, not her grandmother—her chronic illnesses, her hospitalizations, her choice of a husband, her way of bringing out the worst in him, his rages, his drinking, his wishes to be "respected" and pampered, and finally the problems with her children, of which Billy's breakdown was one. She punished herself continually because she felt guilty. She hoped to get some sympathy, some warmth perhaps, some "mothering" from anyone who was available. The fact that it was a son rather than a daughter, and that it was Billy rather than someone else that the problem concerned, could also be explained. Jean was more comfortable with vulnerable men than with powerful ones like her grandfather. She never wanted to be with her husband the way her grandmother was with her grandfather. So she pampered her men and did not mind if they were vulnerable. But she liked them controllable.

More important for Billy, boys identify with their fathers when they are growing up (to the extent that they are allowed to do so), and Billy had no more respect for himself or control over his impulses than his father had. Bill currently was a binge drinker, once or twice a month, but he functioned well and was successful as a salesman. He was the youngest of four children, a "late in life" baby and had a close, "special" relationship with his mother until he was five years of age, when his father returned from the service. According to his mother, he was "hard to handle" as a youngster. The most striking thing about his childhood was his resentment of his sister, who entered her adolescence at the same time his father came home from the war, all when he was five. His older sister seemed to be living out his mother's wish to become a dancer. The mother took her daughter from one dancing school and audition to another while Bill was left to fend for himself. He vied with father and sister for his mother's attention, had school problems as a youngster, went from job to job during adolescence, struggling against authority figures until his twenties, at which time he went to college at night. He quit a few credits short of graduation to take a job as salesman for a small corporation. He had creativity and "good ideas," but "nobody appreciates him," according to his wife.

When two people marry they create a family with strengths, weaknesses, and a style that can be understood in terms of the previous life history of husband and wife. Mr. and Mrs. K. seemed to choose each other as sparring partners. They could justify their anger at each other, his rage at rejecting women and her anger at demanding men. Despite the conflict between husband and wife, this family was together in a powerful and potentially supportive way. It was child-centered, with the children involved in the conflicts, wishes, and strains between their parents. The boys seemed highly prized yet vulnerable, on the periphery of the ingroup, which consisted of Mother and her daughters.

The session lasted a little more than two hours. Billy Junior and everyone else could see that his stress (which led to his overdose after a discussion concerning his leaving home because of his drug use) was the culmination of three years of emotional strain dating from his great-grandmother's death and his mother's depression. Billy's drug use, his "highs," his accidents, and finally his rejection from the family served to distract his mother (whom everyone depended upon) from her pain over the loss of her own mother figure.

"Wow," Susie and Billy Junior both were saying.

"I'm sick. I must look a mess," said Mother.

The therapist responded: "Sometimes being a little sick keeps a person from being sicker or someone else in the family from being sicker. And to get better you have to learn to be a *little* sick or sick in a new way."

"That's a bit much," said Bill Senior. "Let's go over that one next week," he said as he ushered his family out.

The situation described above (an alteration of a true case) represents the kind of work done by a relatively new discipline—family therapy. This case is typical in a number of ways. There is a designated patient—someone whom the family singles out, or who volunteers himself without being aware of it—to divert others in the family from deeper, more painful issues which may then fail to get resolved. It is a device which keeps a family from changing. Adaptation and growth can occur only when real issues are exposed and dealt with. In this case the two therapists began to see Mr. and Mr. K. without the children. Within a month, Billy Junior was no longer depressed and was back at work. Jimmy no longer had school problems. Everyone in the family noticed how everyone else seemed to be experiencing more freedom and more happiness in their lives inside and outside the family. The therapists helped these individuals get underneath the apparent "problem," to deal with the real issues, the "hidden agenda," that had been troubling family members for years, particularly the mother's depression and the father's alcoholism.

Before moving into the main subject of this text—how families can be helped to help themselves—it may be useful to discuss what family therapy is and how it began.

Unlike family counseling, family therapy is a depth therapy that helps all the individuals in a family deal with unconscious issues as well as with "problem patients." It is a clinical specialty (requiring extensive training), practiced by psychiatrists, social workers, and other professionals, in which a therapist helps someone resolve a problem by engaging other members of the family. The problem can be physical or emotional, temporary or permanent. It can be a life-threatening crisis or a "family growing pain." People come together and talk with one or two therapists, usually once a week, for ninety minutes or more. Although the therapy tends to be brief, sometimes involving five or ten such sessions, therapists look upon families not as machines which need fixing but as ongoing, living systems. They see the "problem patient" as someone whose situation involves others in his original or current family. They help the members solve problems by dealing more effectively with each other rather than by turning to ideologies, therapists, or other outsiders for help, except when it is absolutely necessary. They work on the cause-and-effect relationships, the different behaviors, moods, and problems in the family, and all the triggers and cues about which they have little or no awareness.

The approach varies, but the goals of most therapists are similar. They usually include not only solving a specific problem but some kind of family growth as well—better communication, more autonomy, intimacy, or coping ability, and less vulnerability. The effort is to show people how they can be part of a "nurturing family" (as Virginia Satir, a leading family therapist, puts it), or how they can free themselves from a family that binds them destructively. The differences among therapists are more theoretical than practical, and relate more to starting-off points than to destinations.

Some family therapists have psychoanalytic training and use its techniques to show the influence of the past on the present: how people distort their current relationships and challenges to repeat or to "solve" difficult situations of the past. Other therapists focus exclusively on solving a particular problem. They manipulate or challenge the family in ways which lead to problem solving: giving tasks, homework, or even provocations to certain family members. Another important aspect of family therapy is communications and "hidden agendas"—the *real* meaning of the words people use, meaning that can be known only by the *effects*, not the *intentions* of the communications. Messages, verbal and nonverbal, do not simply transmit information; they define relationships. The "how" of communications—"how" people transmit data and expectations—how mother might say "take a coat," for instance, determines the family authority structure, defines expected roles for everyone and divides the family into subsystems: adults, children, men, and women.

Therapists also attempt to learn about the family's past, in order to help members get a different sense of themselves as individuals and to release them from the emotional bind of the present. They help families find a blueprint of their current living family structure in the people, events, separations, sexual attitudes, and challenges of their parents and grandparents.

A common denominator of all the theoretical approaches is the importance of the family and its wider social network. And the techniques are, in fact, an extension of the natural protective and nurturing function of the family.

What distinguishes family therapy is that it enlarges the context of emotional process in time over generations, or in space over the interpersonal field of action. It provides a new ecological dimension to our emotional growth, new techniques to deal with the human environment, and a new awareness as to what that environment is all about.

II

————— ✧ —————

THE HEALTHY FAMILY

THE HEALTHY FAMILY is one that allows people to do and be what they want. It helps them to know what they want both now and for the future. It gives them a sense of security and teaches them how to love. It tends not to produce psychiatric patients or unhappy or unrealistic individuals. It allows people to develop and maintain the tools for relating to others so that they are free, comfortable, and secure in their functioning outside the family.

What does the healthy family look and sound like? Healthy family groups are ones where people concentrate on getting family tasks done without diluting their efforts by getting caught up in emotional business, making points, or proving things about each other. There is a balance between accomplishing tasks and maintaining the emotional and social needs of all the members.

One of the specific features of the unhealthy family is indirectness of communication. When a family functions poorly, members do not communicate effectively. Speeches delivered in the family framework are more common than conversations with any one person. Some members have communication styles which differ drastically from other family members'. They are more silent, require more time to communicate, exchange information less, agree less and in a gross way, seem to fulfill each other's needs less when they do talk.

In the healthy family group clear communication channels imply mutual respect and acceptance of all feelings. Family members hear each other but interrupt each other quite freely; they speak in fragments, usually still understanding each other well. They are aware of each other's experiences, enjoy learning from each other, and are able to solve problems and accomplish tasks effectively together. The family deals openly and constructively with conflicts without avoiding them. Members approach problems optimistically and attempt to solve them aggressively.

Good communication, therefore, implies other things about family power structure and resourcefulness, and individual autonomy, identity, and self-respect. In a healthy family there is little mental invasiveness (mind-reading or members speaking for each other), and members are "permeable" to the statements and feelings of others. Members do not invade the *feelings* of one another.

Each individual has autonomy and takes responsibility for his own thoughts and actions. Each person relates to others as they *are*, not according to the needs, expectations, or past experience of someone else. There is not much blaming except during times of stress (when blaming in small amounts can help spread the crisis around). Respect for each other's views prevents an arbitrary use of power. If feelings are acceptable, and if ambivalence and anger are permissible, members have self-respect at all times and can develop autonomy.

With freedom of communication come negotiation skills and problem-solving ability. If members are able to hear and respond to each other, they can explore numerous options in solving problems. They believe in the complex nature of motivations and emotional events, and can accept alternatives and diversity in the human condition. Agreements are frequently reached by compromise without recriminations if there are mistakes. People can fail without being attacked, rather than the reverse; there is little scapegoating or humiliation. In other words, no individual need fear taking responsibility for his own actions or feelings. Autonomy for each individual is, in fact, expected in these families, and it is built upon a clear definition of one's feelings as well as clarity of communications with others.

How has this picture of the healthy family come to be developed?

Studies based on interviews with individual family members have their limitations because a family, like any system, is somehow different from the sum of its total parts.

In 1975 a group of doctors at the Timberlawn Foundation in Dallas, Texas, combined a number of methods and presented the most comprehensive study of the healthy family to date.

Beginning with an attempt to learn how effectively they were treating adolescent patients who had been in the hospital, they developed techniques that were reliable and valid in studying any families.

They wanted to know what was "interactional, quantifiable, and crucial to the optimal functioning of families." Their book *No Single Thread: Psychological Health in Family Systems* (by Lewis, Beavers, Gossett, and Phillips) is recommended to all students of the family.

The team gave a number of tasks to families—asking them, for instance, to discuss certain disagreements or decide certain issues—and observed their strengths, problems, and degree of closeness with a number of methods, including microanalytic studies using videotapes of family interactions. Among other things, they studied the family's system of authority.

The old rigid power structure of many families used to be matriarchal while the children were young and patriarchal when they grew older. In our time healthy families have a more flexible kind of pattern where there are clear lines of authority, but where leadership roles are interchanged and authority shared.

In the healthy family there is a clear hierarchy with leadership generally in the hands of one parent in alliance with the other, who is the next most powerful person.

Abnormal families tend to be very autocratic or, conversely, to have no leadership at all. Democracy is all right for governments but not for families. The alliance between mother and father is the strongest one in the family: it is the power base. Parents support each other in meeting the child's needs and in handling the child's displeasure, which is part of his growing up. In study after study this coalition between parents has been the most significant finding.

With clear lines of authority there are clear boundaries between generations and there are no strong parent/child alliances. There are strong emotional bonds and satisfactions for each spouse in the marriage. In some, but not all, of the studies there are high levels of satisfying sexual activity between the parents as well. There were often strong needs for the other in each spouse, no overwhelmingly strong competitive trends, and complementary personality characteristics in the marriage patterns. This intense primary relationship with the spouse limits involvement with other members of the opposite sex either in the family or outside it.

In healthy families there is organization without tyranny and lots of role flexibility. Subsystem boundaries are so clear (for instance, everyone is so clear about what adults do and what children do, what men do and what women do) that members will change roles once in a while without feeling threatened. There is a strong tendency for men to be involved in caring for infants and children.

In the healthy family, children are listened to and attended to and influence family decisions. There are infrequent power struggles, and tasks are undertaken with cooperation. The family is not "child-centered" nor is it governed by the "father (or mother)-knows-best" principle. The children do not feel excluded or fearful; they accept their lesser power comfortably. There is at least one parent who is strongly accepting of each child.

In many studies, if both parents were "healthy," so were the children. If both parents were disturbed, the children were also. If one parent was healthy and the other disturbed, then the emotional health of the child depended upon the parental relationship. If it was warm and supportive with a good alliance, the children did well.

The pattern of shared, flexible leadership varies with the task or context at a particular time and becomes a model for relating outside the family as well.

The mechanisms by which early experiences affect relationships later on begin to emerge. Members learn to anticipate that human encounters will be mutually rewarding rather than conflictual in the healthy families. Controls and the need for them relate to assumptions about the nature of man and suspicions about oneself (affecting one's self-image), and one can learn about these assumptions by observing a family's interactions. In less adaptive families, where it seems like encounters will produce anxiety, dominance and submission seem to be the expectation and the pattern both in and out of the family. Sharing the power seems to be too risky for these people.

The healthy family seems to expect good things from encounters with other people; they have Erikson's "Basic Trust." They also trust each other and learn to see each other as separate individuals, learn to express themselves and ultimately feel empathically for each other. They are open and honest in agreements and disagreements. The power structure, therefore, does not prevent communication and growth; rather, it provides a medium for it.

In disturbed families, members are always fighting or they never fight or there is no closure or resolution to a conflict. The amount and manner of conflict is less important than the tolerance and coping ability in dealing with problems and resolving them, which again depend upon flexibility, good communications, and a tolerance for feelings of any kind. In healthy families, there is a certain distance with availability between all. Members are allies, respect each other's view and disagree in conflicts rather than deprecate each other. They tolerate the biological drives, bodies, feelings, spontaneity, initiative, and uniqueness of each individual family member and endorse the involvement of each one in activities outside the family.

Dr. Robert Beavers, a member of this team at Timberlawn, presented a composite picture of three different types of families: troubled, mid-range or adequate, and healthy.

Seriously troubled or disturbed families are repetitive in their interactions, clinging to each other with little involvement with the outside world.

"Adequate" families, on the other hand, have rigid controls. People avoid change and feel threatened by biological drives of members. They avoid stress from the outside. Whereas in disturbed families children had serious problems, in adequate families no one was severely ill emotionally, (though wives were frequently unhappy). When younger members in these midrange families did have difficulties, the type of problem depended upon the family structure. When the youngster was close to other family members he tended to have neurotic problems.

Neurotic problems occur when there is emotional suffering inside the self. There is a clear sense of reality and sometimes good functioning, but there are high levels of anxiety, fears, and problems with obsessive thoughts or depressive feelings.

When the young person was separate from this kind of family, he became vulnerable to a different kind of maladaptation called behavior disorder. This is where the young person gets into trouble by doing things. Usually he begins by becoming troublesome to other people, and later he feels troubled himself. Rather than experiencing emotional suffering inside himself, he spreads it around. One finding was surprising: The crucial (and really only) difference between the poorly functioning and adequately functioning families related to their feelings about themselves and their commitment to the family. The adequate families had high levels of self-esteem in members, valued the idea of the family more and reached out and were involved in the community more. Seven out of eight other variables comparing these two kinds of families—for instance, those concerning parental alliance, levels of conflict, and communication patterns—were otherwise similar.

Healthy families carry their structure "lightly," and concentrate on accomplishing tasks, meeting and adapting to change actively. They are flexible in structure, and again, the single most important feature was a marriage that met the needs of both parents. They are families with high levels of activity and initiative in reaching out to the community.

As individuals, fathers in adaptive, healthy families who were no more successful at work than those in adequate families, focused more on their interpersonal satisfaction than on success at their jobs. They were also more supportive and closer to their wives, who expressed marital and family satisfaction. Women in midrange families frequently expressed unhappiness and had psychosomatic problems or weight problems or depression more often than wives in healthy families.

The children in these two groups were more alike than different, healthy and competent as far as this study is concerned, despite pain and struggle in the family. Regardless of problems of their own, therefore, parents in adequate families can produce healthy children.

In addition to talking about communications and power structure, Dr. Beavers described other features of the healthy family. Regarding separation and independence—a dimension highly prized in our society—the members of the healthy family think, feel, and act clearly as separate individuals early in their interactions with the family and can become autonomous later on without much difficulty.

Healthy families allow individuals to accept the reality of death and separation. No one is indispensable. People die and they are buried—literally and emotionally—and life goes on. Having separated psychologically from the mother during infancy in the normal way, they construct a family system that can adapt to loss and change. Family members do not depend on unchanging relationships in an unchanging world. In mourning they do not hold on to loved ones living in the past or in a timeless fantasy world. Here again a strong parental relationship allows adults to break away from their own parents, which sets up good generation boundaries—an example for children on how to deal with separation. The other characteristic of healthy families that allows for autonomy, separation, and the ability to handle loss is a meaningful relationship and attachment outside the family.

Many healthy families have a "transcendent" value system or commitment to a group or idea that allows the person to reach beyond himself and his loved ones. Possibly loss of meaningful religious ties in today's society makes adults cling to their children more. Many children reciprocate (although they seem to run away from their parents, ending up "away but not separate"), unable to build families of their own. They are in a certain kind of limbo, separated, single, or "swingle," some living in communes and others devoting their energies to cults of various types.

The healthy family's sense of reality and judgment of them-selves coheres with that of the people around them. There is no attempt to deny painful realities when they occur and to avoid problems. Members' feelings and thoughts are understandable to skilled observers, normal outsiders, and family members; this, despite a high incidence of interruptions and spontaneity in communications. No emotions are intolerable or disclaimed, so that individuals take responsibility for their own thoughts and feelings without feeling vulnerable. Such a pattern enhances a member's sense of confidence in his own mental processes and his perception of reality. Although there are family myths—shared beliefs about the family members and their position in the family that go unquestioned—these myths do not distort reality percep-tions and are similar to outsider's views of the particular quality of the family. Members are quick to respond to change and to pain in any individual member.

In emotional tone, healthy families tolerate a full range of feel-ings and encourage expression of them with no threat of being overwhelmed. The prevailing mood is one of warmth and affec-tion, and there is empathy, sensitivity, and responsiveness to the feelings of others. There are no particularly unhappy subsystems, no long-lasting depression among the women, loneliness among the men, or feelings of oppression in the children. Negative feel-ings toward one another are made with full awareness of the other as a separate person who can be supported and valued even as he is criticized for one or another *thing*. Open expression of feelings and freedom to come and go become coupled with a sense of self-worth in each member. As can be expected, there is less conflict and much less irresolvable conflict in these families. No argument limits the range of future interaction or threatens to cause dis-integration of the family.

In brief, good communications, shared power, individual au-tonomy, good reality testing, a sense of the passing of time in the human life cycle, and warm and expressive feeling tone charac-terize the healthy family.

The family is an open living system. The way a family is organized is both cause and effect of how well its individual members function. As the world changes, as people grow, the family changes. And even the most rigid family structure has a range of possibilities. All families have been in the past, and can be in the future, different from the way they are at any one moment in time. Individuals need only be aware and learn about themselves and their families in order to take some measure of control over the way they respond to growth and to change.

III

─────── ◦ ───────

EXERCISES
IN UNDERSTANDING
YOUR FAMILY

Hᴏᴡ ᴄᴀɴ ᴡᴇ ɢᴇᴛ to know ourselves—not just on an intellectual level, but on an emotional level—in an enduring way through our families? Should individuals address themselves to the family around them (if there is one) or the family that is still living within them, that defines or constricts or ennobles them in their own lives in the present? What kind of work can they do? How far can information take them toward awareness—and awareness toward fulfillment? Who can benefit and who cannot?

All human beings are products of a sexual transaction between two people, and of a childhood that shaped their adulthood. Although every person is unique, all human beings share in certain of these universals more than they differ in specifics. Such a realization of the humanity in all those around us and before us gives us perspective on information about our families, past and present. We can build on this knowledge, develop empathy and emotional awareness within ourselves, to fulfill our potential for health, pleasure, and productivity, and to help those we love fulfill theirs.

We know that if one person in a family starts functioning better, sooner or later (usually after a few storms) the others will too. Growth and identification processes will ensure that children are affected positively, while emotional contagiousness and feedback mechanisms will ensure that other adults are also. We know finally that there is another kind of "reverberation," that healthy families produce healthy, adaptive societies.

The exercises that follow are guides to two kinds of voyages which every person can take. First, there is the voyage outward into the past to understand the unseen structure of the family that shaped us as individuals, how it came to be, and what it means for us now. Second, there is the voyage inward to get to know the different selves inside each of us—the emotions that go along or fail to go along with the many different roles that each of us has. By believing in our own uniqueness, by deepening our emotional awareness, and by practicing with others in our families, we can gradually become free, here and now, to expand our resourcefulness, heighten our pleasures, and enhance our capacity for intimate relationships.

DIAGRAMS

A GENOGRAM is the most common kind of family diagram; it outlines family members and the most significant events: births, deaths, marriages, and divorces. Circles represent females and squares represent males.

Children in order of age follow:

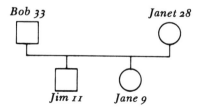

Significant events and variations are a part of the diagram as simply and clearly as possible. For instance, twins, one of whom died at birth, are indicated as follows:

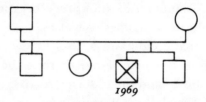

Deaths are shown by an "x" with the date

The diagram is then carried up into the families of origin of both parents. Genograms are like upside-down trees with the roots on top. (Place, dates, and occupations can be added if you like.)

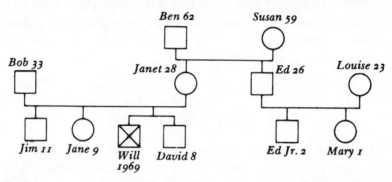

As the story of the family's history over time is told, alliances and splits as they developed can be drawn in. Although it is a still picture, a mere blueprint of a dynamic, moving entity, the genogram can be helpful as a starting point—a fixed foundation for the family structure. Seeing who was raised for whom, as a replacement for someone in the older generation, or as a gift or ally or sparring partner, or enemy; who resembled whom in sex, physical appearance, occupation, and sibling rank; who sided with, or fought with whom—all can give a sense of proportion, a perspective concerning the origins of roles, and a direction to individuals in the current family. The balance, the richness or lack of it, the course of domestic events, how well each child does and in what context, the number and sibling order of brothers and sisters in each family, the tolerance of each for both sexes, can all be seen in the splits, coalitions, and life course in the family genogram. In most families, one sex thrives better than the other, and the emotional tone that surrounds all, especially minor children, is important in determining each member's view of the world outside.

What was happening in the family field during the conception, birth, and first five years of each individual? Emotional forces impinging on a person, designating him or her for a certain role, are as powerful as physical forces and as precise as electromagnetic ones.

With the genogram as foundation, one can construct a dynamic living history of one's family by learning details: the concerns, the character types, and the milieu of each family's times. What occupied and preoccupied these individuals, what threatened them and what gave them pleasure? What were their economic, cultural, and sexual lives like? How did they care for each other? How did they communicate and how were decisions made? Were there painful separations? What was it like to be a man or a woman in these families?

Answers to many of these questions can be found by almost everyone through records, birth, marriage, and death certificates. Every group, for hundreds of years, memorializes these events for its members as a way of defining itself. And, despite Depressions, migrations, and Holocausts, records are more available and enlightening than most people imagine.

Other sources for such information are people who remember or have heard about one's forebears. Relatives, partners, friends, and functionaries of every kind (teachers, students, bridesmaids); anyone who might remember what the people and the families were like can function as tribal historian, since most of the facts and much of the history can come from written sources. There is probably inaccuracy and distortion in such hearsay reports, but distortion exists in every person's view of every family situation. It exists in a description of family life in the here and now, so it should not be surprising that it exists in memories of families of the past. The more sources one finds and the more information one gets, the closer one comes to important truths about one's family.

Dr. Murray Bowen, the eminent family therapist, advises people to go "back, back, back; and up, up, up" the family tree to look for patterns, "recycling," getting not just information, but a feel for the context and milieu that existed during each person's formative years. Diligence and patience first bring surprise and sympathy for those half-dozen families and dozens of individuals who played a part in making us what we are, where we are; but later they bring a sense of release from locked-in feelings and situations. Dr. Bowen advises people to focus on their own mental and emotional state in doing this kind of work. The more one is *comfortably related* without being *emotionally entangled* with family members on every generational level, the more healthy and productive one can be in one's own life in the present. Alex Haley, in *Roots*, searched his family tree and like many other Americans found the emotional roots he had been looking for in the ancestor who made the journey to America, an eighteenth-century African slave forefather. The glory of *Roots* is that it traced one wish, one idea—the wish for freedom—back generations, kept alive in the family structure and mythology.

Citizen Kane's last word, "Rosebud," revealed what his life had been about—a search for the safety and pleasure of his childhood and loving father figure (all symbolized by his sled, Rosebud, from which he was ripped away as a boy).

The search for a father is perhaps the foremost theme in American life and art, from *Huckleberry Finn* to Johnny Cash's "A Boy Named Sue," and probably relates to American mobility, aggressiveness, and the drive for success.

Mark Twain overcame a crisis in his life as a writer, when he was unable to finish *Huckleberry Finn*, by going back to Hannibal, Missouri, where he grew up, and to the Mississippi, where he worked as a steamboat pilot. The sameness and the change in both the place and within himself in some way freed him to continue his work.

It may be true that "You can't go home again" to be in the world as it was in the past, but each of us can and must go home again in order to fully understand and know ourselves, and to free ourselves in the present.

How can this trip home be approached? In general, go to people to find a place in the past, and to places to find people. Also, most families or groups that have extended out have periodic get-togethers in addition to marriages, births, funerals, and the usual rites of passage for individual members. These reunions are rituals of a sort that serve not only to initiate new members but to touch home base, to see, feel, and hear the other people in a context of which one is a part. These gatherings are like weekend reserve meetings, people checking in and out, communication lines being tested. They can also be an opportunity to learn more about grandparents and great-grandparents, people who are gone but who created the structure that can be seen in the various families that have descended from them. Try to learn what their lives were like, their challenges, their decisions. Usually, the more one-to-one conversations you have, the better. The common past shared with other family members gives a perspective on your life in the present.

These gatherings become opportunities also to rework old emotional business between yourself and others. This is not just to settle old scores but to see, feel, and learn how others are handling their lives and the changes that have occurred within them over the course of time. You get a different view of other members of the extended family that is sometimes at odds with the fixed image in your memory. These get-togethers can be emotionally difficult, even overwhelming. There is no better way to learn about a potential spouse than to go to one of these family affairs. For the most part they are valuable and necessary parts of family living, providing a security and a perspective that can be exhilarating.

Those without families eventually feel the pain of their isolation for lack of such an attachment. It is no coincidence that the suicide rate is frequently higher on Christmas Day than on any other day of the year. Reunions of all kinds, not just family events, are opportunities for growth, but family reunions, even between two members, can be especially so. It is not the blood relatives but the people who were important during our early years, who shaped us and whose experiences are part of us, that we should seek out.

Many family therapists ask individuals to bring in parents and grandparents, people from the old town or the old street, to help families understand themselves, regardless of the problem and who has it at the moment. The therapist usually tries to guide a renegotiation in the same way that one can do by oneself at family gatherings. For the most part, individuals in our culture are well advised to go to every family event they can—births, funerals, christenings, circumcisions, confirmations, etc.

People are also well advised to take as much time and deliberation as possible with family crises—deaths, births, and other significant events—and work feelings through to avoid aborted emotional reactions. These aborted reactions will affect your functioning, your decisions, and your judgment, only making for new problems that are built on unresolved feelings. People frequently decide to marry or divorce or to go into a new business shortly after the death of someone they love, especally if they are back at work in a day or two and seem to be "getting over" the loss very well. Later on, they usually regret decisions made during this period. It is easy to understand why the Chinese figure for "crisis" is the same as the one for "danger" and for "opportunity"; also why, according to ancient Chinese legend, men go away from their work and their families for *seven years* when their fathers die.

Arthur, for instance, was deeply depressed when his father died. He loved his wife and children and his work, but nothing had the same zest or pleasure that it had while his father was alive. They had been in business together, and had shared jokes, joyous experiences, and some difficult times. Yet Arthur felt he had never really known his father, who had been a powerful man, loved and feared by many. He was well read and knowledgeable and had an irrepressible sense of humor. Early in his life he had had religious training, had studied to become a rabbi, and later studied law. Yet he had also been a prize fighter, a gambler, and a union organizer. Like everyone else, he was a mixed bag of loyalties and identities.

All his life his father's approval meant more to Arthur than anything else. He wanted to help his father and to make things easier for him. And his father, a powerful, successful businessman, seemed omnipotent—not in need of anything Arthur could give, and at times he even seemed unreachable.

In high school, athletic success, popularity, and girl friends;

later on, money, children, and success in the business—all were mediated through his father. And he did make his father proud. It was always as if his father had been hurt in some way and Arthur had to make something up to him. He had never told his father he loved him, and he regretted that more than anything else after his father's death.

After a year or so, Arthur was less depressed but still seemed somewhat withdrawn from life. One day, as his son looked wistfully at him. Arthur remembered an evening thirty years earlier when he looked at his father the exact same way, reaching out for someone unreachable. In this moment Arthur knew what he was searching for. He wanted to know about his father's life. To understand would be to recover something, enough perhaps to allow him to get on with his own life. Besides, there was some mystery about his father's life. Something just did not add up.

Arthur went to Israel to talk to friends and relatives who knew his father's family.

Grief does not vanish in three weeks or six weeks when we lose someone we love. The acute pain ceases, but we rearrange our inner and outer lives, and our new self stands as a monument to the person we lose. Furthermore, we do not grieve simply for a person when he or she is gone. We grieve for the things about the person that connected us to him or her. We grieve for objects, for aspects of relationships, for things we liked and things we disliked. We grieve for a pipe or a pair of slippers, we grieve for someone who protected us or whom we wanted to protect. We grieve for a memory, a place, a business, a customer, a sound, or even a smell. Sometimes we do not even know what it is that we grieve for.

Arthur's father was a Russian Jew who came to join his father in America when he was twelve. He always spoke lovingly of his father and of how he missed him during his boyhood in Russia. His father came from an intellectual and esteemed Orthodox Jewish family. Educated as a rabbi, Arthur's grandfather came to New York and worked in a garment factory, sending money back to Russia to support his family. That was all Arthur knew.

One night, after arriving in Israel, Arthur attended a gathering of a group of relatives and friends that came closest to what Arthur could call his "clan." After a delightfully heavy meal of mixed

Jewish, Israeli, and Arab delicacies—laced with heavy doses of chicken fat, chickpeas, and olive oil—Arthur's inner boiler began rumbling, his intellectual fires were hot, and he began asking questions.

The questions concerned Grovna, his father's hometown in the larger state of Grodna. Israelis, however, prefer violent political arguments to discussions of geneology. "Grovna?" Uncle Ely asked. "Go see *Fiddler on the Roof*." He got up and walked out of the room.

This was a nonverbal communication that Arthur recognized instantly. It was one of his father's and his American uncle's favorites: to get up and walk out, only to return, say something, and walk out again.

Something like musical chairs, it was more a conversational "search and destroy" mission. They used verbal flamethrowers. They would burst into a room, spit out their comments, and flee.

It was endemic to his family rather than to Jews as a whole, and Arthur began to feel he was getting somewhere. The women were less fidgety and more knowledgeable, and they stayed in their seats and began to talk about the "old country."

There followed the usual discussions of boundaries and dates.

"It was Poland then in 1917, not Germany."

"No, it was Russia, then Poland, after Germany; not Poland, then Russia."

Then they discussed sanitary conditions, the outhouses. They talked about little Martin, Arthur's father, and his devastating use of his American flashlight at night around the outhouse.

Finally they got around to the families, to Martin Carl's childhood and relationships. Martin's father, Herschel, had gone to London.

"London?" Arthur asked. "I thought to America."

"Of course, to America," his aunt said. "That's why you're American. But first he went to London."

"And he sent for David and Martin," another aunt joined in. "They came to him in London for a while, and then they all went to America."

"How long a while?" Arthur asked.

"How old is your Aunt Sarah?" another aunt asked.

"Sixty-eight," said Arthur.

"And your father, he should rest in peace, would have been—"

"Seventy-three," Arthur answered.

"Then his father was in London and America for three years."

"Away from his wife?" Arthur asked, innocently.

"If he was in London and New York and she was in Russia, yes, he was away from his wife," Uncle Ely said. "You know, we had no choice about these things."

"We had choices," Aunt Irina corrected, "but they were difficult choices." She raised her finger as she spoke, another gesture Arthur knew.

"Then they came from America back to Grovna. When Rachel was born, Herschel went away again to America. Your father went to study with Rabbi Peritz."

"He lived there, didn't he?" asked Aunt Irina.

"Sure," Uncle Ely responded, "when you study with Rabbi Peritz you live with him. Your father had some brain. Everybody knew it. A rabbi he should have been."

"He went right to university in America," Aunt Irina pointed out. "No high school."

"He spoke like an Englishman."

Suddenly Arthur understood his father's speech, something he had never known about before. His father had some mixture of an accent, not Yiddish or New York, where he grew up, or European or English. It was a blend, one ingredient of which had been elusive.

"Rabbi Peritz always said that 'Moishe'—that's what he called him—'some brain he's got.' But he had his hands full with him."

"Hands full?" Arthur asked.

The men laughed.

"He was a wild animal."

Arthur was insulted.

"A wild Indian, he means," said Aunt Irina. "A wild kid from America. He was what you say, a delinquent, a tough guy."

"Wait," said Uncle Ely. "Didn't he live with Moishe Capoira?"

There was a silence suddenly in the room, as if they all seemed to feel a closeness. Most of them smiled. Those who didn't were holding back a tear. It was the same look people in New York had when they talked about Martin, how he did things and what he meant to them.

"Ay. Moishe Capoira. Sure, Herschel's brother. Your father lived with him two years before he went to study with Rabbi Peritz and to yeshiva."

"That's where he learned to be a wild Indian," said Aunt Irina.

"Herschel and his brother fought like cats and dogs, yet they loved each other."

"Moishe wouldn't leave Grovna. He was too happy there. He looked like a Christian, with blond hair and blue eyes. Wait, Moishe Capoira and your father were named after the same person, their uncle who died when he was a child, he should rest in peace."

"And they both loved Herschel."

Back in czarist Russia, Moishe Capoira used to say he was in show business. He was a "magician." He would "go out in the morning with a rope and come back with a horse."

"He stole your father's flashlight, American flashlight," Uncle Chaim said, "and tried to sell it back to him, but he met his match. Your father tried to burn his house down."

"Juvenile delinquency," Arthur thought. "Here it was sixty years ago in czarist Russia."

"But they became great friends. He taught your father to play cards, to smoke cigarettes. They stole horses together, smuggled people over the border."

"Delinquency; a czarist Fagin." Arthur was thinking. Arthur heard about the relationship between the two Moishes for an hour, and the relationship each had with Herschel, the family "star."

Finally, Chana, the oldest, told about Martin's departure for America. "When he left, he said good-bye to everyone. His mother and sisters would follow him to America. He said good-bye to all of us, to Rabbi Peritz, but when he said good-bye to Moishe Capoira, he cried."

Arthur had never seen his father cry.

"He cried and cried, and he went off to his father in America."

Here was the piece Arthur was searching for, the part of his father that was always missing. Arthur cried himself, as he understood the "search for the father" that came down through the generations in his family.

Dr. Bowen guides people in their renegotiation with members of their families of origin in a most specific way. His approach is consistent with his theory of family process, perhaps the most well-formulated, comprehensive theory offered to students of the family. According to Bowen, each person has more or less autonomy or independence in his thinking and feeling, and an intellectual as well as an emotional side to his psychological self. The end result is that every person has a greater or lesser degree of "differentiation of self" from others in his family relationships and past generations. The independence ranges on a scale from those lower down who are fused or "glued" or connected in their psychological functioning with their families of origin and later relate to those in their new families the same way, to those higher up who are more or less autonomous in their psychic functioning. The "differentiated" self is solid, stable, uninfluenced in its wholeness by relationships with others, although it allows the person to be flexible in his feelings and resourceful in his behavior.

The other important concept in Bowen's theory is called "triangling" (or in therapy, *de*triangling) and calls attention to the universal phenomenon in human culture and relationships of the trinity, or triad. Two people in an intense dynamic relationship tend to reach out and effect a third person in some way, by inviting or rejecting or communicating through or complaining to or giving birth to this third party. Freud found the Oedipal triangle; Gerald Zuk, the family therapist, uses the third-party-as-"go-between" concept. Bowen feels that people exist as members of a three-part system, and that the more anxiety or tension that exists between two people, the greater is the tendency to draw a third into the relationship, changing the balance between the three members. When things are calm, there is a comfortable twosome and an available outsider. When anxiety is high, the outsider has the preferred position until he is drawn into the field of tension, allowing someone else to have more distance. There is a consant state of motion between all three members of the triangle, and movements are usually made automatically and without awareness. The more "differentiated" one is, the less anxiety and vulnerability one has in these triangling moves. One can then be more aware and in control—primarily with a goal of not being drawn in, leaving the two people in conflict to work out a solution that is less anxiety provoking. For instance, if Father complains to Sister about Brother, and if Sister agrees, she and Father become close. If she defends Brother, she and he are close and Father is the outsider. If she refers Father to Brother in a specifically neutral, friendly way, she is distant enough from both, remains the outsider, and Father and Brother must work out their problems.

These two concepts, encompassing (1) emotional maturity and autonomy, and (2) the view of families as a series of dynamic triangles are the basis for an effective system of therapy and a format for the work of researching the family in the service of one's emotional growth. Dr. Bowen advises people to go and see family members and avoid doing "the same old two-step that you always did when you visited before, but try to get a real person-to-person relationship with them." You should have specific purposes in mind during visits; for instance, getting information about ancestors in order to get new perspective and control in situations with people where you may have felt less in control before. The content of the interaction is not as important as the style and the use of the self that emerges during such visits. You should respond to others by developing a plan such that, despite emotional involvement, a certain degree of awareness is always present. You can and should plan a strategy to avoid being drawn into triangles in the family that only allow the two other family members to get off the hook. They should respond to the tension by working it out between themselves, and not by drawing someone else in. You should not respond in a way that leads to continuing the conflict, to any ploys that threaten to entangle you. You should talk and listen, and focus on what is going on inside yourself emotionally and intellectually as a result of the changing interaction with the people outside. Remaining aware and in control of your own sense of self, while still maintaining emotional contact with family members in going over old business or family history, can be a powerful experience—one that can set off a chain reaction, giving everyone more emotional breathing space and enhancing your capacity for familial intimacy and pleasure.

I HAVE OUTLINED how an individual can explore the forces affecting him—the designations and roles he is expected to play, usually without being aware of them—by understanding his or her family system historically.

How can each person approach the part he plays in the system in order to solve problems here and now and continue to grow inside and outside the family? The first and foremost rule in family living is that each person should focus on himself, on his own way of reacting, thinking, feeling, and behaving. What am I doing and saying in my behavior toward others? How do I appear? Can I see myself as others see me? How can I know more than just what is on my mind? What is there in my feelings at this moment that I am not immediately aware of but I know must be there because of the situation and my knowledge of myself?

Each person plays himself in a family as each member of an orchestra plays one instrument. Focusing on others is like being a violinist trying to play the piano with a violin bow. It interferes with two parts in the ensemble and, at best, brings silence. There are rests and pauses in our emotional lives and there is a time for listening, but the music comes when each one plays his or her own instrument. Judging, fearing, manipulating, hating, controlling, placating, avoiding, or denying the wholeness of others eliminates both "I and thou" in relationships. Needing or wanting someone else to be different, and spending time at the task of changing him, is letting yourself off the hook. By knowing and working with yourself, you invite others to play their parts in the family ensemble.

Knowing is not enough, although it is the first step. You must work to feel feelings and resolve them, and use emotional states as a musician practices his scales. All feelings are okay. People should never feel guilty or responsible for their feelings or thoughts. They are responsible for their *behavior*—the manifestation of their feelings.

If a person is angry, he can do any one of a number of things:

He can swear, spit, cry; he can slug the person he is angry at; he can slug someone else who may differ in sex or in size from the person he is angry at; he can think about the anger; he can try and forget about the anger, or he can let his body react to the anger for him. The more he knows about the feeling of anger and about himself, the better off he is, and the less the anger will disturb his functioning or his future.

People learn how to handle feelings very early in life. They learn what feelings are shameworthy by watching and experiencing the reactions of the people around them. Children who are told, "Never get angry at little sister," or "Don't be afraid," or "Don't cry," get the message about what feelings are okay to show in their families and what must be hidden.

Intimately connected to a family's tolerance for feelings is its tolerance for people, and the child's self-esteem depends largely on how he is valued by others. The child gets the message by the reactions of others—their availability and respect for his feelings and needs, including the need to grow, to be frustrated and be separate, eventually to become autonomous and leave the family. The child should need mother and father less and less as he grows, and this should be tolerable for all concerned. When this process goes awry, problems arise later in life, and people come to have the rigid needs and expectations of others that they had earlier had of their parents.

At this time in our culture these difficulties can commonly be traced to certain trends that do not seem on first glance to go together: abandonment and gratification. Children are abandoned by parents who are caught up with their lives in the world outside. Children are also deprived of manageable amounts of frustration, and it is frustration that allows one to grow. Parents often are overly connected and envelop children, leaving them no room for autonomy. They gratify the child but do not work with him in his growth. Or they concentrate and obsess on child rearing and feel the child's tears or frustration as a reflection of their performance. Often, because they are emotionally exhausted from such concentrated efforts, they require vacations and periodically abandon the child, so that the overall message is one of inconsistency.

Self-awareness begins with self-knowledge about your family

background and your own childhood. The important considerations relate to how comfortable you were and are with feelings and how you handle all the emotional experiences of family living, including dependency and growing autonomy of children; separateness from parents, spouses, children; male and female sexuality; anger, and loss. What did you miss in growing up in your family of origin and what are your sore points? After thinking about it, you can then proceed to feel it, to work on yourself, to try and get to know in a deep way what your feelings are, what you do with them, and what alternatives you might have in handling them.

Virginia Satir works with people to increase their awareness of themselves. She links tolerance and comfort with feelings, to the individual's basic sense of self-esteem—the most important ingredient in making workable relationships with others. When a person recognizes his own uniqueness, he can tolerate and respect himself, give to a relationship, and know what to expect in return. The failure to become whole enough to be separate as a child comes out in a failure to be free later on as an adult, and the problems in relationships can take any one of a number of forms. Satir uses a series of exercises to put people in touch with themselves and with their ways of relating to others. People have a number of ways or styles of expressing their need to stay connected to others: they can do it by blaming others, usually their spouses, or by placating them, blaming and denying themselves. They can also walk a tightrope in relationships, maintaining a fixed distance from others in their lives, becoming uncomfortable or hostile with closeness. They fear perhaps that they might be swallowed up or even go crazy if they let their guard down. The styles are easy to observe or depict nonverbally. There are those who point their fingers at others, those who point to themselves, those who stand with arms folded, analyzing all situations, and those who are "out of it," or uninvolved.

The choices we make are usually not conscious ones; they are the results of experiences in early life concerning how we related to others in order to feel comfortable, lovable, worthwhile, and in control. Those who learned to blame others spend their lives making a good case for themselves as if life were lived in a courtroom. Those who learned to sacrifice their own wishes so that they can never be accused of asking anything for themselves; those who function like computers, always in control of their feelings (the one they can acknowledge) ; and those who become detached from others, issues, or even reality, all live out the agendas of their families of origin. There are trial lawyers, martyrs, computers, and infants. Blaming, placating, and ignoring are the red, yellow, and blue of the emotional rainbow out of which all other interpersonal attitudes can be derived. The common denominator for all these styles of communicating is that one does not allow, experience, or express a feeling and respect oneself for it.

Role playing, an exercise that family members or strangers can do together, is a way of experiencing the constriction of these kinds of interactions. Three, four, or five people agree to discuss something, any topic will do, for five to ten minutes, and one person will blame the others at every opportunity, another will constantly blame herself or himself and never give any thought to his or her own wishes. A third will constantly analyze the situation without relating in a feeling way to anyone else, while another might be detached or as irrational as possible. After the exercise, people talk about what they experienced, usually revealing a sense of constriction and a wish to run away. The feelings become quite real because most people know what all these feelings are like. Most of us have played all these parts at one time or another in our lives, and the exercise can heighten our awareness of different styles of relating that go on in families.

COMMUNICATION

GOOD COMMUNICATION begins in self-knowledge and self-awareness. Rules to "say this" or "do that" in a relationship only work when they become part of the self-concept and when they affect a person's mood and his sense of possibilities about himself. People get to know themselves by learning to listen to themselves, to look at and feel themselves. Many therapists say that if you know your feelings and can remain comfortable with them, your feelings will not control you, *you* will control you. A person must learn to go freely from inside self to outside self, into relationships or the world outside without changes in his self-image or psychological functioning. The observing and controlling self must never be overwhelmed by the feeling self, but must integrate it with the needs of the moment. Insight is born of this capacity for awareness when dealing with the challenges of growth and change that life provides. You will ultimately be able to see yourself as others see you and see relationships as others see them.

Yet awareness and understanding are not enough unless they are integrated on an emotional level. It is always true in human relationships that feelings will out. Years ago, comedian Shelley Berman joined Mike Nichols and Elaine May in a routine on television. Shelley Berman played a husband who came home unexpectedly and found his wife, Elaine May, in bed with Mike Nichols. The confrontation, after momentary embarrassment, was followed by the most polite, rational, and civilized discussion imaginable between all parties concerned: a decision to divorce, an instant property settlement, and warm feelings between one and all. They then decided to drink a toast to the new arrangement and Shelley Berman mixed martinis. He took great pride in his recipe for martinis and so informed the others. Mike Nichols sneered, took a sip and was horrified—he thought the martini was terrible—too warm, too sweet, "effeminate." Naturally, the criticism turned into heated discussion, discussion became an argument, and finally one of the men drew a pistol and killed the others on the spot.

Because we are all human and emotional, we function to a great extent on an unconscious level, and instructions or wishes to change in a certain way do not necessarily affect the way we behave. Because the family is a system, however, when change occurs in one family member, even though it is at first resisted in others, it will eventually produce changes in others, creating a new family emotional balance. For this reason, in clinical situations family therapists work with whomever they can reach and affect, rather than the "designated patient." A conscious change in one person can affect another person's behavior and feeling state, even though the other person's behavior has roots that are temporarily or permanently beyond his awareness. Knowing what families are all about, we can understand why one change can trigger off others, reverberating throughout the system.

FEELINGS VERSUS THOUGHTS

BEFORE LOOKING at the signs and signals of good and bad communication, which are really only a way of keeping score, it is important to know the rules and purpose of the game. Good communication begins in knowing which "you" and what part of you is relating to the other, what part of the other is really there and what part you are creating.

It is necessary to know the difference between thoughts and feelings. People frequently say, "I feel he should be more loving," "I feel she should be more self-sufficient." These are thoughts, not feelings. What both these people probably *feel* is anger. Feelings include love, rage, anger, fear, or sadness. Rage, annoyance, and frustration are different varieties of anger. A thought is something in the head—an idea, an opinion or judgment, or a series of ideas that add up to a fantasy. A feeling is a part of your whole being, sometimes "felt" in the body. Thoughts are easier to know than feelings. When you know yourself—the kind of person you are, your past history, your sore points—you can approach the context around any given moment in time and be prepared for the present. When you have an awareness of your feelings, you can work for freedom and new options in creating yourself and in creating other relationships.

Every relationship is a hall of mirrors. How can we know which image is a reflection—someone from our own past or a part of our own self-image—and which is the real other person? Select someone with whom you have an intimate relationship and with whom you sometimes conflict. Think for a moment of what it is that frustrates you about this person. Did you ever know someone else whom you perceived the same way, who seemed similar, or who aroused similar thoughts or feelings in you? Did you ever link the two of them in your mind? "That's men for you—all thoughtless." Or, "Women are like that." Behind classifications of any kind there are frequently past images.

Next, thinking very specifically about all the things that frustrate you in your partner, were they ever or could they ever have been true about you? Finally, think about how your partner has changed during the time of your relationship and how these changes have affected you. Now you are prepared to work with each other on communicating.

Communication between people is defined as the sum total of the messages given to the other with words, silences, or acts of any kind that affect the other. There are two kinds of communications: those dealing with an issue or information or task at the moment, and those used in the service of emotional business, creating or reinforcing images or needs or roles that people have of one another.

A family ship is seaworthy in proportion to how much communication is above the water line (task oriented) and how much is below the water line (emotional business directed toward others in order to prove something, to get something, or to get even). To inspect your family along these "lines," start with yourself. What would others say about your own sense of security and your self-esteem? Next, think about how comfortable you are right now in your family. Now you are ready to begin listening to yourself and to the other members of your family.

What do you talk about and for what purpose? What would be most gratifying as a result of your conversation—a well-planned family event, a new personal resource, or someone else's admiration or admission of guilt, inferiority, or need? How do you view others when you relate to them? How fixed and how flexible is your image of them and theirs of you? How often is conversation to enlighten yourself and others, and to change a situation for the better? Communication is known by its effect, not by its intent and certainly not by the words involved. Most people usually speak of love and their own innocence, yet criticize each other endlessly. Criticism usually is designed to hurt or subjugate the other, seldom to change him. If saying something once or twice does not work, why say it again? Criticisms are usually repetitive and come out semi-automatically because they serve some hidden emotional purpose for the critic and his object.

RULES OF COMMUNICATION

PSYCHOLOGIST Sven Wahrloos's excellent book, *Family Communication,* and Dr. George Bach and Peter Wyden's *The Intimate*

Enemy are among the many books about communication in families, and I recommend both.

The following rules can be used as a way of knowing how well you and your family relate to each other; they can also be used to change communication patterns. Such changes in behavior can set good things in motion in the family, not forgetting that enduring change is always more likely with increasing self-knowledge, awareness, and work with one's family of origin.

1.   Concentrate and listen to yourself and others in communication. Think about your verbal and nonverbal messages to others. Look at the effects of your communication and that of others on you. Focus on yourself before you focus on others. Get to know your feelings—how they affect you, your mood, your body, and your productivity. Accept all feelings as honorable.

2.   Think before you talk. In communications, "automatics" fire "dumb-dumbs."

3.   Don't say "never" and don't say "always." You are then dealing with a fixed portrait—a still picture—constructed by yourself that is largely irrelevant to the dynamic family situation and to the *possibilities* in all the others in your family.

4.   Be as positive as you can, especially with children. With adults such communication is a lubricant for relationships. It will serve best to get you what you think you want. (If you are unable to be this way, you probably do not want what you think you want.) With children this positive approach forms the basis for their self-image and capacity for good relationships later on.

5.   In arguments and heated discussions, do not talk about the past. Do not respond to an accusation with a counteraccusation. Do not exaggerate or respond to exaggerations. These are all short circuits, mindless rituals, signals that there is no real communication. If you hear these going on, start back at Number 1. And good luck.

IV

THE FAMILY UNDER FIRE

THERE WAS A TIME when, if someone asked us who we were, we would answer with our family names. "I'm a Chase." "I'm a Leon." "I'm a Lombardi." And our answer was illuminating; the inquirer knew something specific about us from our reply. Now the question, implicit or explicit in every introduction, is not "Who are you?" but "What do you do?" This shift says something very clearly about what has happened to our attitude about the family. There was also a time when Americans used to think about individuality, spontaneity, and independence, and the enemies of these traits were governments and authority. Now we talk about independence, spontaneity, and individuality, and the enemy is the family. Everywhere the family is defamed and repudiated.

Anti-family feeling reached its peak in the sixties, when the family became the scapegoat for society's ills. All authority was under attack, and all of our institutions were subjected to scrutiny and redefinition. The affluence of the fifties led to the radical intentions of the sixties, (just as the depression and dread in the wartime forties led to the affluent fifties).

We live in a country that was built on a set of ideals (including individuality, independence, equality, and freedom) based on a strong moral, even religious, puritanical foundation. There was a powerful barrier against authority and intrusion from outsiders, especially governments. In contrast to conditions in Europe, Americans lived in a land of plenty, and this permitted a new, nurturing, mother-child relationship that helped create individuals of spiritual strength. Americans were able to forge a strong family structure and an independent spirit.

Founded on a political rather than a religious ideology, family life in America was a new development in Western civilization. Early in our history, families were separate but not isolated, linked by their common immigrant status and by political beliefs. Society had a structure based on the preservation of various freedoms, especially freedom from interference by governments. There was distance between families, largely a reaction to constraints that had grown up in the crowded, complex, authoritarian European societies. Because it was an immigrant society, people came one by one and found themselves alone in the new country. They extolled the virtues of individualism and formed partnerships easily; for protection, efficiency, and companionship. They fought with each other, shared with each other, and even rescued each other; but Lone Rangers all, they avoided commitments that would interfere with survival, success, or mobility.

Rural living encouraged large families and self-reliance. Children, because there were many of them, were less attached to their parents. They worked for the family and made companions of particular brothers or sisters. Although life was precarious, there seemed to be a minimum of despair or helplessness. People were aggressive and ambitious, and through their efforts they had a good chance to achieve all or part of what they wanted. The value system and the new family patterns led directly to the political events of 1776, perhaps the most inevitable War of Independence in history.

In the nineteenth century, with migration as an entry point to American society, there was an exaggerated boundary between parents and children. Freedom from oppression and from government was matched by a freedom from Old World values and from one's heritage, embodied in parents.

Young immigrant Americans frequently were raised by their siblings and peers. Cut off from the Old World, cut off from their parents, new Americans, like their forebears, became travelers, with a sense of the land rather than a sense of any one particular place. A wandering breed, they created their own states and, later on, their own towns and suburbs. They viewed America as a land of promise. Second-generation Americans sensed their difference from their parents and, in effect, raised their parents in the new American style. (Third- and fourth-generation Americans reversed this focus and searched for their roots, identifying with grandparents and great-grandparents whose view of the world and way of relating to intimates were concretized in family structures.)

The self-sufficient nuclear family, unencumbered by government, heritage, or kin, separate from but cooperative with neighbors, whoever they might be, was highly functional in the immigrant migratory society. "Future Shock," as described by Alvin Toffler, was not just a product of technology and the Industrial Revolution but has been with Americans from the first migrations. Trading posts became towns, then cities; railroads changed wastelands into crossroads communities.

The main effect of Future Shock on the family was the separation of generations. Because of the rapid change and continuous challenge that was perhaps the most common theme everywhere in American life, parental styles of adaptation no longer worked.

It was, however, the rise of industry that changed living styles definitively and created the modern American family. Increased specialization broke the family up by requiring different members to be in different places. Fathers worked outside the home; the children no longer learned a trade from him but went to school. By the time they grew up, need for their father's skills might have vanished. At home, daughters no longer learned from their mothers. And as time went by, each generation became less housebound. Technology changed how women spent their day, and though they were less affected than men by developments outside the family, they were affected by changes in the family.

In earlier times, with sharper generation boundaries, and cut off from other families as well, husbands and wives were often close and dependent on each other for involvement and gratification. But now with the separation of roles ouside the home, sharing was sometimes a problem because one spouse might be unfamiliar with the other's activities. Marriages founded on romantic love can deteriorate later because of the failure of a partnership to develop. A partnership depends upon contact and togetherness, familiarity with each other's lives outside the family, and, to some degree, even a potential for taking over aspects of each other's roles. Marriages of young adults in love, in other words, change over time, and the presence of children in the home requires spouses to be parents, to be different as individuals from the way they are as husbands and wives, and different in their relationship to one another as well.

Children in these new households grew up cut off from their parents. The natural alliance between a father with his son and a mother with her daughter failed to develop. The secure togetherness followed by the gradual separation that makes for healthy identification was interferred with. Nowadays we see men carrying a lifelong yearning for a father, women for a mother, and a vulnerability in the marriages that these individuals make later on.

Men become "workaholics," success addicts spending day and night with colleagues, all in their search for this closeness with a father that they missed out on. Women feel lonely, depressed, in need of tenderness, all in their search for a mother. They are disappointed in their spouses. Men are contemptuous of women who are not powerful or precise or independent ("manly") enough. Women find their husbands lack tenderness or "understanding" or softness. They are searching in their spouse for the parent of that sex, usually as a reaction to becoming parents themselves.

A result of the Industrial Revolution was that it put pressure on the nuclear family, the very structure that was best adapted to meet the needs of technological society. There was too much specialization and too much separation between family members. Functions that were originally within the family—educational, religious, medical, and protective functions—were now performed by society, but society cannot do *all* the things a family can do.

Families were becoming more and more adaptive, but individuals were falling apart.

The effects varied with the time and place. Economic depression kept families together, although it kept them in an atmosphere full of threat, while the affluence of the 1950s and '60s created more separation between family members. Recently, in American society, emotional vulnerability has replaced economic vulnerability. There has been a reaction against specialization and sharpness of sex roles, and choices are being made more frequently on an individual basis.

Our dissatisfaction with our lives—our boredom, our despair, our disappointment—starts with this increasing isolation of families and individuals. Our modern culture is mobo-centric and few of us establish lifelong roots. Most of us can say "where we are from," yet we often wonder where we will be next. We cling to identities, labels ripped out of context, like white, black, Italian, Jew, and WASP, without knowing what they really mean to us. Rapid transportation and communication have brought an increased homogenization of society. Middle-class families of today resemble lower-class families of the sixties in regard to child abuse, broken homes, and depression. About 200,000 infants and children will be abused by their "caretakers," according to Professor Urie Bronfenbrenner. Psychiatrist Robert Coles points out the similarities between middle-class families, with their isolated, nomadic life style, and migrant families. Atlanta, Peoria, and Portland are beginning to look more and more alike.

With increasing wealth on a world-wide basis, increasing financial and life-support systems available to lower socioeconomic groups, and ever-increasing taxes for the middle and upper classes, there is vertical as well as horizontal "homogenization." There are fewer and fewer neighborhoods, and not many of us have a sense of identity beyond our families: no ethnic, religious, or political identity that has pervaded our life and has endured. Relationships with kin are optional, and children and adults spend most of their time socializing with peers. Parents work away from the home. Father spends an average of fifteen minutes a day in direct contact with his children; mother, fifteen to twenty minutes a day directly communicating with them. TV has become the "eternal light" in

many American homes. With their parents lost somewhere outside in the affluent society, children feel deserted and are soothed
with objects; toys and TV, endlessly gratified, never satisfied, and
the cycle perpetuates itself down the generations. Cut off from our
past and our parents, we "discover" adulthood and middle-age
crisis as something new. Separate from grandparents, we deny
death, but read thanatology.

Children have less contact with adults, their parents or other
adults, than they used to. The 1970 White House Conference on
Children gave the reasons: "A host of factors conspired to isolate
children from the rest of society. The fragmentation of the extended family, the separation of residential and business areas, the
disappearance of neighborhoods, zoning ordinances, occupational
mobility, child labor laws, the abolishment of the apprentice system, consolidated schools, television, separate patterns of social
life for different age groups, the working mother, a delegation of
child care to specialists—all these manifestations of progress operate to decrease opportunity and incentive for meaningful contact
between children and persons older or younger than themselves."

This new world of isolated human beings brings new discon-
tents. Cared for at schools from a very early age, educated by peers
and by TV (up to fifty hours a week of it for preschoolers), children receive a double message from parents: We care and we
don't care. ("Don't bother us but make sure you tow the line.")
We require them to give little to the family until later on during
their schooling when we expect them suddenly to compete successfully, to "perform" and be mature simply by virtue of their
age. Children follow the example of adults, and many of them—
more than one million per year—run away from home. The rates
for suicide, accidents, crime, and unemployment for young people
have increased dramatically. Only academic ability has declined,
as measured by college board and aptitude tests. This is not so
much because of poor schooling but because of poor preparation
and commitment to education in their families. Schools clearly
cannot do what families should do. Moreover, there is confusion in
the home about how and when to get help from the outside.

In the malaise we feel and the desperate rhetoric we hear calling for new "openness" and "growth," we come to understand

again how we have applied old solutions to new problems. We guard against oppression and conformity while our lives lack structure and a common value system.

The new heterogeneity in life styles, the "pluralistic revolution," is more than a reaction against this increasing homogeneity; it cries out against the isolation people are feeling, the sense of vulnerability and abandonment despite refrigerators, TVs, and adequate incomes. And it cries out for a consensus of values, especially in intimate relationships, responsibilities, and parenting. Is success as important as we think it is? Do we believe those who say they don't care about it? What are the different kinds of success and what price we do pay for each? Do we value our own feelings of competitiveness more than feelings of cooperation, and which do we encourage in our children? Should we be structured or permissive with them?

There is not as much pride in being a parent as there once was. People have children to "get it over with" and resent parenthood being forced upon them. Many of us are still fighting old battles with our own parents, within ourselves and through our own children. There is no new Dr. Spock, and people have mixed feelings about the one we have, some blaming him for the malaise of a whole generation. Our freedom hangs like a weight around our necks, most of all for young people who, as psychiatrist Herbert Hendin points out, more and more often "grow up dead," becoming suicidal in late adolescence. Having destroyed the oppressors, we are now alone. We confuse emptiness with freedom, isolation with independence, madness with transcendence.

One of the enduring changes of the radical sixties is the women's movement. Many women have turned away from the stereotype of the "stay-at-home" wife and mother. They have rejected the mythic nuclear family as an oppressive institution. Other women continue their efforts at self-definition and are ambivalent. They cannot reject their families; they remain caught up in choosing between oppression and loneliness. Following their example, men too have begun to question their own ideas about "masculine" conventions. Moreover, our value system, which places higher priority on success at work than in the home, makes men feel lonely and women feel secondary.

People with more time, more money, and more options have built on the American tradition of individuality and have demanded more and more freedom of choice and expression. They have created the "new narcissism" of our present age as freedom's response to "homogenization," conformity, and boredom. We know that moral and emotional development take place within the family, and we have seen what today's families are like. The family reflects the value system of our society as it was created by citizens of today and their families of yesterday. If intimacy and commitment are seen as oppression, and families as reactionary, people become overwhelmed by too many options and retreat into the self. Or they reject themselves and their bodies and join new armies to defend one or another particular belief or path—cultist, dietary, psychological, or pseudo-scientific.

Born as a secular society with an ideology rather than a religion as its base, we languish now because we are without a transcendental value system, even as our children search far and wide in the world and in themselves for a different kind of consciousness. The hunger for answers and for structure, the wish to "escape from freedom," as Erich Fromm termed it years ago, can be seen in the thousands who joined Reverend Moon, Hare Krishna, and some of the many therapy movements. It is a reflection of the crisis in values that exists in our society today.

The eternal verities like truth, justice, and love, and even the American verities like fairness, honesty, and generosity have given way in our time to a struggle for success. Mad gamesmen, we compete for prizes that change every generation: money, status, and more recently, style. The prizes vary with the times and with our view of others outside our families and what we need from them. Again, our goals reflect the boundary between family and society and our ability to trust and work with others. We structure our families to turn out competitors. Many of us live to work rather than work to live. Others of us work at finding different pleasures. Efficiency, performance, and "bottom line" are our watchwords.

Our families are stratified; parents are with colleagues and children with their peers. Our children reject us when they become adolescents as we reject them when they are young; they learn little about family living and are ill-prepared later on for marriage and parenthood. The old, the young, and the infirm are frequently outside the family where they can be cared for "properly" and not impede us in our search for the "Golden Fleece." What we fail to realize is that this increased efficiency changes the notion of the family for all of us, even if we currently happen to be the "healthy," independent members. We delude ourselves that we live only for the moment. We lose track of time and of our world as it was and as it will be. We are all infirm every day. Our world changes every minute, and it is only our world view through our families, past and present, that helps us keep our emotional forces in balance.

The old are removed into gray ghettos or golden ghettos or nursing homes by virtue of one characteristic: age. The wisdom, the experience, the clarity of vision that comes from the long view of things, the balance, the control, the lowered vulnerability to excitement to which younger family members can become addicted, could be invaluable in decision making and in maintaining emotional perspective in families. It is not because nursing homes are five or ten times more expensive than living at home, or because people are healthier and happier and more able to function living with kin that we should avoid such isolation. By keeping older people out of contact with families, removed from the living, we just prolong their deaths. More important than any of these factors, however, is that *we* and *our children* should keep in contact and maintain a sense of the life cycle of which we are all a part.

The old are isolated from the young. Men are isolated from women. (The women's movement sometimes brings them together as competitors.) With no sense of the family life cycle, we keep solving the problems of adolescence: finding a "one and only love" and deciding about our work, what we want to do when we "grow up." We solve one set of these adolescent problems in our thirties and a whole new set in our forties. With a longer life span for parents, their children remain children for a longer time, perpetual adolescents struggling to be infants. Deprived of togetherness early, many never learn how to love, and they spend their lives in a lifelong search for a substitute, endlessly trying to find a comfortable distance from others, afraid of closeness and afraid of loneliness. Denying the need for togetherness, family members impose it on each other by making one another feel forever guilty and responsible.

Life-cycle events such as childbirth, illness, and death are handled with isolation, efficiency, and dispatch so that we are not disturbed. Yet we simply pass our "solutions" on to the next generation. Separation at childbirth, for example, can affect the mother-infant relationship and other relationships in the family as well. Premature babies who are kept in incubators seem to get more child abuse and fail to grow normally much more frequently than other infants. Child abuse, according to Dr. E. James Anthony, is ten times more common in babies who are delivered by Caesarean section. The child is more vulnerable in these families and so is the relationship between his parents. Divorce is five times more common in families where babies are removed from their mothers immediately after birth. The first postnatal contact could almost be called a human imprinting phase. The early closeness between mother and infant seems to be necessary. It protects both mother and child and affects the family forever afterward. Early isolation, which occurs so frequently in our society, seems to prepare the way later on for isolation and stratification in the family, and a warped togetherness with a confused, inhumane value system outside it.

We blame the family for much of our discontent. We hear that the family is weak, dying as an institution; also that it is powerful but evil, the root cause of our modern dilemmas. The fact is, any enemy can be found in the family precisely because it is the foundation of our society. Despite what we hear, however, the family has been neither destroyer nor destroyed; it has only been defamed. And spiritual renewal requires respect and understanding for a value system and for the family that teaches it.

To effect change we must learn not only about ourselves but about our institutions as well. The family and society are different institutions, and society is no more a large family than the family is a microcosm of society. Still, they are both complex "open" systems. Society, like the family, adapts to change and moves from one crisis to another. In all systems there is a resistance to change and it occurs with difficulty, and change in one part implies change throughout the system. We can expect, therefore, that in social institutions, change occurs slowly. It also requires a certain ferment or instability. Adjustments in attitude reflected in new laws and in new codes usually occur only after larger, more drastic possibilities have been discussed. Put another way, revolutionàry talk produces reform and social change; rigidity and intransigence produce revolution. If tension in a system is not dissipated, it builds up to a point where it can destroy the system.

The family changes in its own way and at its own pace, and the general direction has been toward increased specificity of function. Nowadays, for instance, sexual relationships are less automatically linked to marriage, and marriage does not automatically include having children. There has also been a dramatic increase in the number of blended and single-parent families. Now one out of three children lives in such a family.

Moreover, in recent history people began marrying for love and emotional satisfaction rather than out of need.

Current trends continue in the same direction, according to sociologist Talcott Parsons, with increasing specificity of the different functions of marriage; also with increasing expectations, choice, and variety in family living. Specificity and variety do not solve all of our problems, however. People complain about loneliness when they are single, suffocation and disappointment when they are married. Dr. Otto Pollak puts it bluntly: "There is marriage and there is singlehood but there is no free lunch!" The need to work on our lives and know the ramifications of what we choose remains.

Despite what the media and our "crisis chatter," as Saul Bellow terms it, seem to suggest about the death of the family, most Americans have not altered in any major way their style of living. For instance, regarding alternative life styles, although many Americans probably know what "open marriage" is and are interested in hearing about it, most do not practice it, let alone consider it a norm. And what we consider the norm is as important in the evolution of our institutions as how we behave. Our attitudes and feelings are part of what we do; they inform our behavior. They affect the communication and identification processes that are crucial in families, especially for children. Our ideas about norms not only help us define where we are, they tell us our direction for the future. The interest in alternative family life styles implies a dissatisfaction with the family but not a repudiation of it.

Lately, people have been examining and challenging limitations from inside themselves rather than from outside. Our puritanical heritage was obsessed with the control of sexual wishes, channeling them according to dictates that originated outside but which ended up inside the self. We attributed these dictates or inhibitions to the family, and they not only forbade incest and extramarital sex but also affected our ability to enjoy our bodies in a more general way.

We are no longer obsessed about the evil of sexual pleasure. Contraception and treatment for venereal disease produced a sexual revolution. And when sex is no longer dangerous, it is no longer evil. Individuals began to enjoy a range of pleasurable opportunities outside their families. Many people now are sexually active before marriage, and since marriage is viewed as a changeable institution, some continue experimentation after marriage as well.

The new generation would work to limit other "evils," such as acquisitiveness, inequality, and isolation—"evils" that stem more from the outside than they do from the family. We have shifted from concern about controlling our sexuality to concern about expressing our emotionality, from guilt over sexual impulses within the family to guilt over aggression outside it.

Yet, despite the sexual revolution, we have discovered that there is more to intimacy than sex and that emotional commitments are complex. According to statistics, most people in our society have, or hope for, satisfaction in intimate relationships and in spite of experimentation with alternatives, family life offers the most stable framework for it.

Nevertheless, our nuclear families, overburdened and isolated, are sometimes unsatisfying. Just as prolonged stress reactions in the body create illness, especially when the stress is gone and the reaction to it continues inappropriately, the highly functional and adaptive nuclear family, which got us through an industrial revolution, two world wars, and an economic depression, has become dysfunctional in this time of affluence. We are bored, stressed, confused, and lonely. The new hedonism and the "new narcissism" we experience are reactions to the consumerism and the conformity of our parents, and the Depression, and displacement of our grandparents. We suffer from *solutions* to problems of our parents' and grandparents' generations. Protected from *their* struggle, *their* Depression, *their* war, *their* Holocaust, *their* dread of diseases which crippled whole populations, we lack *their* capacity for intimacy and love, *their* sense of triumph and self-respect.

The repudiation of the family we hear about is born of the needs of a new and different society, and expressed by individuals with unresolved feelings toward their parents and others around them. It sounds like the imposition of new norms, but ultimately becomes a link between generations and leads, for most people, to a wish to explore new options. Living together, for instance, is a common practice, entailing sexual commitment and a more gradual, precarious emotional commitment. The arrangement is often the secret dream of the parents of today's adolescents. It is done, young people say, solely for the pleasure and the practice of the two people involved and implies no gesture toward society, leaving no room for intrusion from others. All options are open for the future. Living together without marriage is a reflection of the real evolution of the family as it continues today.

I think it is naïve to repudiate the family because of the trends and conflicts we struggled with in the fifties and sixties. The family is not simply the rigid, mobile, self-contained nuclear family that was designed for efficient functioning in the forties and fifties and that is still alive in our fantasies, mostly as an object of scorn or nostalgia. The family is more than this. It is an idea, a series of loyalties, a shifting, evolving group of permanent attachments. The family is the sum total of all the relationships, functions, attitudes, feelings, actions, ideas, memories, and loyalties of all the family members, as individuals and among each other. It is paternal and maternal, changing and immutable. While our styles and ideas about marriage change every generation, the requirements of parenthood are constant. The family is eternal. If you look at the families around you, perhaps you will see, as I have seen, the many new and varying family structures—flexibly extended, one-parent, and blended families that people are fashioning for our times. The literature repudiating the family is a rejection of the family only as an unchanging structure in a changing world.

V

THE FAMILY AS A LIFE-SUPPORT SYSTEM

Happy families are all alike;
every unhappy family
is unhappy in its own way.

TOLSTOY

A FAMILY IS a small group of individuals, usually related by blood or by law, who have emotional bonds of a particular kind with one another. They care for each other and are committed to each other. They express their caring the way they learn to in their families, and the result of their caring is that they help one another adapt to the changes that time and the world outside bring to each individual. The style of families therefore varies more than the purpose.

Family members have a stake in each other's welfare. Events that affect one affect the others. As a group, they share a common history and a common purpose, and if they do not live together in the present, they have in the past, or they might in the future.

The family provides a place where they can be with each other in an intimate way. It provides a safe harbor, a "home base," a place to "let your hair down," a place where, as Robert Frost put it, "when you have to go there, they have to take you in."

The basic functions of the family are twofold. As a place where the welfare of one affects others, where one can *be* certain ways with safety and the protection of others in the family, it is a place for being without doing, for immaturity and "regression." It provides for the emotional and physical needs of its members. It keeps them in an emotional equilibrium, psychologically fit, helping them to function better in the world outside.

The second purpose of the family follows directly from the first. As a protected environment which allows immaturity and physicality among its members, affectionate caretaking as well as sexual kinds of physical contact, it naturally becomes a place for raising children. It is a place where the young can define themselves, where they come to know what it means to be a man or a woman, to be young or to be old. It provides a medium for them to grow into stable, adult members of society, eventually to leave the family of origin and start families of their own.

The family exists in every known society and civilization, and can even be found among primates and mammals. It is the building block for the society around it, and family members survive as individuals only as well as their society can adapt to the world outside. Man is a group animal, in the prehistoric or in the modern corporate hunt, and families are the life cells of the group.

Families respond to a society's needs by changing their structures, specifically their membership, lines of authority, alliances of different subgroups, and spatial configurations—that is, how separate and potentially independent members are from others. And families respond to these changes not immediately, but over time, according to the built-in biological time clock for human growth and development. Because the growth needs of family members are more or less constant, there is a time lag between requirements of society at a particular time and the fixed physical and emotional development of individual members. This time lag makes the family a powerful buffer, mediating demands and urgent purposes of the society, so that family members are not overwhelmed. It also saves us from our societies. Our social institutions are changeable and potentially dangerous. And it is the family with its buffer effect that saves us from ourselves—our civilizations, our "solutions," and our ideologies. It eliminates our Hitlers. It changes the goals and dreams of a Ghengis Khan to those of Kubla Khan, his enlightened grandson. It is impossible to overestimate the importance of this family mechanism and the biological safety-valve effect it produces.

Notwithstanding the isolation of the modern nuclear family, one still cannot speak of a "normal" or "healthy" family without speaking of the society outside. The adaptable family will vary with the adaptation and "health" of the culture around it.

With this perspective one can say, therefore, that there is no normal or perfect family. There are family organizations with people who are more or less adaptable to any given culture. We can now understand Tolstoy's meaning. Happy families are ones that provide members with a framework for living, a ship for traveling comfortably within a particular culture. They go more or less smoothly, even during storms or times of stress, and the individuals are able to cope without requiring too much from others outside the family to maintain their equilibrium.

The job then of the family is to create individuals who can help the society to flourish while ensuring the survival of the individuals. Put another way, families create people who create societies that influence the families.

Understanding this concept is crucial to our adaptation. As products of our families and creators of our society, we have two tasks. We must respect our families and understand and work on *ourselves* through knowing our families. We must also direct our efforts at change toward society, toward the family as a *societal* institution.

Only by knowing ourselves can we address ourselves to our society effectively. When we get a sense of the interaction of the systems involved—between the individual, the family and society —we realize how it is impossible to talk about one system without knowing about the others.

In the family, children develop identities as members of a group and a sense of themselves as individuals (a first and a last name, as Dr. Salvadore Minuchin, the leading "structural" family therapist, puts it). The family helps each member deal with crises or steps in his growth, all of which can be felt as change or separation. Each individual affects the family in different ways, and successful change is blended into the group and subgroup structure. All the major internal tasks are derived from the primary one of early psychological separation, leading up to autonomy and physical separation from the family later on.

From a systems point of view, one looks at the family in terms of its structure; that is, its members, roles, boundaries, coalitions, inner and outer space, and how this structure is affected by internal change, family life-cycle events, and external change.

Family "structure" is invisible and can only be known from the ways that family members interact. Through subtle communications, verbal and nonverbal (and the choice of words as well as the content is important here), one can recognize the roles, relationships, power structure, and subgrouping of any family. Who talks to whom and how, defines relationships. When mother says, for instance, "Have some fruit," she says it in a certain way to her husband, who responds in a certain way, and differently to a child, who reacts in *his* own way. This kind of interaction repeated over time defines who she is in relation to others in the family. The subsystems have different tasks and out of the tasks come roles, individual identities, the capacity to learn, and personal flexibility. For instance, child rearing is the job of one group, being children is the role of another. Each subgroup can be further divided; for instance, the older sibling is told, "You take care of things while Mother is away," while someone else is always known as the "baby."

Each subsystem functions best without interference from others. For instance, negotiating with peers requires freedom from one's parents. Learning to negotiate with Mother requires freedom from Father. Tasks are accomplished one at a time and each requires a specific posture from others in the family. The goal is to accomplish them while continuing to grow in one's personal skills, and it is best achieved in an atmosphere of independence with cooperation.

Clarity of boundaries is more important than who is in each system. As Robert Frost put it, "Good fences make good neighbors." Rules like "Don't go into Jimmy's room between eight and ten at night"; "Don't go in without knocking"; "No sleeping in Mommy's and Daddy's bed"; "Don't lock the bathroom door." All these rules define boundaries around and within the family. Boundaries are the framework of all families and determine the distance between members and the overall functioning.

Too much communication and involvement, with blurring of the boundaries, diminishes the distance between individuals. The boundaries are diffused and easily overloaded, and the family has lots of overreactions, emotionality, but poor resourcefulness. This kind of family pattern Dr. Minuchin calls "enmeshment." With too much distance between people, and rigid boundaries, family communication is decreased and the protective function of the family is inadequate. This pattern is called "disengagement." It becomes the "every man for himself" type family. In Woody Allen's movie *Annie Hall*, the two different kinds are superimposed on the screen in a memorable dinner-time scene. In one family, everyone talks, eats, and breathes over everyone else; in the other, members are set apart, conscious of the distance between themselves.

These different types of families are neither good nor bad in themselves, but they lead to different kinds of vulnerabilities for the individuals. The more enmeshed the family is, the less is the autonomy of its members. The personal skills of children will not develop well. In the disengaged family the "independence" frequently is emotional distance. Individual members cannot ask for support.

Boundaries also determine the degree of "reverberation" in the family, how much anything that affects one member affects the others. Sometimes the more a particular stress can reverberate or be "spread around" the family, the better for the individual. Enmeshed families overreact to stress, and disengaged families do not buffer the individual enough. As we saw earlier, often the best thing a therapist can do is to be a boundary maker.

The nature of society is important here, and one of the ways in which societies affect family structure is in boundary formation. With an inhospitable or dangerous society outside, as experienced in the past, for instance, by Jewish or Sicilian or Early American frontier families, there is a clear, powerful boundary between the family and the outside. Family members are close and individual subsystems are blurred. Families feel the world as a "them" against "us" situation.

In addition, distances in the family depend upon the individuals involved and their particular life stages. Early in the child's life, the mother is close to him or her. Later on, when the father is more engaged with older children, the mother is released. Families are structured to minimize stress at any one point in time, and they tend to resist change and maintain a pattern once it evolves. Yet they must be flexible in order to grow.

"The problem, Doctor, is Sally." Mother was speaking gently but emphatically. Sally sat on the couch next to her mother, poised, smiling sadly, her head erect. Sally had run away from home. "This child hangs around with her so-called friends, hanging around street corners . . ." The mother was in tears. "The whole family is waiting for her to come home, we like to have dinner together. She just doesn't know how dangerous it is around Front Street there. This child . . ." "This child" was a physically mature beauty of thirteen.

"I go to Alcoholics Anonymous," Father was saying. "I haven't missed a meeting in three months."

"We go to Alateen, Charlie and me," said Sally. She looked sad, almost as if her beauty implied some kind of loss for her.

"I've been dry since February," Father was saying. "I've been drinking since I was eighteen years old."

"Wasn't that when Sally ran away the first time? February?" one of the therapists asked.

"That's right," Mother and Father were saying. "That was enough for me."

"He's been very good," Mother went on. "He slipped a little at Susan's last month, but you've been very good. I've been around drinking people all my life. My father was an alcoholic."

Mrs. J. was born in Europe, the oldest of eight siblings. During most of Mrs. J.'s childhood her mother was ill, and she died when Mrs. J. was fifteen.

"I had to take care of my brothers and sisters and cleaned up after my father. I have been working all of my life." Mrs. J. was tearful. She looked older than her thirty-seven years, overweight and short, close-cropped hair, with a gray dress.

Young Charlie was looking at his mother and then turned to Sally. "She does good in school," Charlie was saying. "National Honor Society."

"It seems like just yesterday she was in the Brownies," said Mother.

The therapists asked Mother and Father to shift their seating arrangement. They put Mother and Father closer and facing one another. Sally was moved down nearer Charlie on Mother's side. Mother continued: "I was eighteen when I got married and worked right up until Sally was born."

"What was it like for you when you were Sally's age?"

"I was too busy to go out. There were seven kids in the house and I had to feed them. We were real poor. Next thing I knew I was on a boat coming to America. My aunt was here."

"How was it leaving the Old Country?" asked a therapist.

"It was hard. I cried. My mother's buried over there. I want to go back."

A trip back sometime in the future seemed like a good idea.

Parents' complaints about teenagers and adolescents' complaints about their parents' restrictiveness are normal turbulence for most families. Sally was a child in a new, adult body that changed everyday. She had a new power, a desirability, and she needed to find out many things about herself and the world that she would not be able to learn through her parents. They would not be able to tell her, and even if they could, she would not be able to hear. She needed her friends and her school; she needed distance without being endangered.

Learning to deal with rebellion, negotiation and sex education had not been Mrs. J.'s strong points in growing up. Pleasure was secondary to survival for her and her siblings during her childhood. With a sick mother whom she loved and needed, and a father who drank because he needed his wife but was angry and powerless to help her, Mrs. J. steered her family ship. She was grateful for the security that she now had. She had solved the problem of poverty which terrified her so as a child. After years of serenity, however, her past caught up with her in the form of Sally and her "problem." And the crisis in the family could be an opportunity for both women to learn to enjoy their femininity and even their sexuality.

"What do we do, Doctor?"

"Let's start with little things. Dad, instead of learning any more dances from Sally, why don't you teach Mother the dances you already know? Sally, you dance at the school dance."

One therapist wondered about Mr. and Mrs. J.'s sexual relationship and asked about sleeping arrangements. Mr. and Mrs. J. slept together; Sally and Charlie each had their own rooms. He asked how often Mr. and Mrs. J. went out, what they did, and how they enjoyed it.

"Charlie," another therapist asked, "how would you like things to be different at home?"

Charlie smiled. "I'd like to go places with my father. Hunting, fishing, shopping, downtown." Anywhere seemed good enough for Charlie.

Sally, the original "patient," was outside the circle, which consisted of the therapists and Mr. and Mrs. J. She was no longer somber but had brightened up and looked calm and alert. Sally stopped running away after this session because she was no longer so uncomfortable in her family.

This case is a good example of how families can solve problems by "restructuring" their activities in very specific ways. Sally found she could get more distance without having to run away, the two men in the family needed to become allies, and Mother was less depressed because she got support from her husband and the therapists.

The relationship between mother and father (the "spouse subsystem") is the first and the most important one in any family. It is a mutual support structure that provides examples for others in the family. Based on mutual caring and identification with the other, the spouses learn to give in to each other without giving up any part of themselves. The process between them makes the family greater than the sum of its parts. The identification with parents and their relationships, both between each other and with others outside the family, is the basic growth mechanism for children.

The willingness of a young adult to give up separateness from his family of origin in order to belong to a new family is the first task of marriage. Insistence on "independence" in family members early in the game is often simply an inability to accomplish this task. Becoming a member of the new partnership enhances the possibilities for each individual, but it awakens old feelings toward intimates from one's childhood. As this regression sets in, both partners will appear to change, and new agendas might emerge. Some will insist on "improving" or "saving" the partner. Others will make new standards and be chronically unsatisfied. It is no accident that the highest rate of separation and divorce is in the first year of marriage. If mutual caring can transcend the anxiety inherent in commitment and closeness, if each spouse can *trust* enough, the marriage can endure and grow according to the needs of each.

Although the same two people are involved, the parental system is different from the marital system. There are new tasks that must be incorporated into the family without upsetting the accomplishments and satisfactions of the marital relationship. With the birth of a child, there are three new systems: mother and child, father and child, and the new family.

Mother and baby are close. Father is more distant, and he often finds mothering qualities within himself in order to get close to mother and child.

Later there is a sibling system, which provides the child with his first peer relationships. He learns to make friends and enemies, to support, scapegoat, compete, cooperate, and get recognition all in the context of his play with brothers and sisters. There are older and younger siblings in a generation, and the first and second siblings have different family systems to deal with. Children learn to deal with peers and later on with colleagues outside the family the way they deal with their siblings. When you wish to know how someone will function in an organization or as a business partner, find out about his early relationships with brothers or sisters.

When the child separates to go to school, there can be a new stress that challenges all the individuals involved. As the child functions away from the family, the family changes. School is a test for the parents of how well they have managed their task of child raising. It is a new line of communication, a new input from society to the family, and it is sometimes felt as an intrusion. If a family is eccentric, there are limits as to how much contact there will be with those outside the family, and this becomes most noticeable when children start school. It is a time for exposure, not only for the child but for the whole family system. Societies vary in their degree of tolerance, and if the people outside the family in a particular class or ethnic group or area of the country have a high tolerance for diversity, the child who is special can move out with less of a problem.

School phobia is the classic problem of families who are overwhelmed at this stage. It is the fear and dread of school, and it is treated sometimes by child psychiatrists who help the young person overcome his fear, and at other times by family therapists who see the parents, helping them recognize the challenge and feelings that school brings to them, as well as their unspoken messages to their child about their own fears and expectations.

In school the child requires challenges that he can respond to, he develops a sense of mastery, and he practices social skills that he learned earlier while relating to siblings or playmates. He learns to make independent decisions and develops different identities in relation to peers. He is a leader with some, a follower with others, and he tries to develop talents that his friends will value.

The pre-adolescent, as in the case described earlier, emerges from her peer group to become aware of sexual wishes and a new potency for acting on them. She must cope with physical changes and a new body image, sexual attractiveness as an adult, and the loss of a certain security she felt as a child. Sometimes other family members are threatened by this new powerful adult who might be prettier than her mother or taller than his father. There is a growing distance between the young person and her family, whose atmosphere vacillates from one of conflict when she is close to one of loss when she is distant. The adolescent looks outside her family for peer support, ideologies, heroes (who may include teachers, athletes, and rock stars) while she develops social skills—this time with the opposite sex. Adolescents fall in love, experiment sexually, and come to understand new sides of themselves and their potential as adults.

At length, if she is able to step out into the world on her own, pass whatever test she feels is a measure of her usefulness, she can then feel a rapprochement with her family, adult-to-adult, without being threatened by old feelings of dependency and regression. Satisfaction at work, school, and in relationships in the world overshadow the temptation to be a child again. It is important that she really leave her family, detach herself from it and test her mettle as an individual, not in an ephemeral, uncommitted way, but separate and alone in order to experience the change within herself. It is only then, detached from the old image of family members, that she can make new relationships with new images of each of her parents and be ready to fashion a new family of her own.

Specialization of roles with flexibility is the backbone of the "good enough" family structure. There must be clarity about the roles, and the simplest and the easiest way (although not the only way) to achieve it is for different individuals to fill them. The absence of clarity or fulfillment of these roles, either through accident or through conflict between members, or disturbances in the personality of the parents, can create defects in the family structure and can affect the younger members who are developing a sense of their own identity and learning social living.

Since the child grows by identification and internalization, he observes and interacts not only with other individuals but with the family system itself—its relationships, feedback mechanisms, and other styles of handling emotions. It is important to understand this concept—that the child does not simply internalize mother or father but aspects of specific relationships and attitudes of individual family members. A family can have one parent or two parent figures of the same sex; it can be with or without siblings, relatives, and other specific family members. Yet the child can grow up and emerge whole and well adapted. Nuclear families are not the only healthy ones, and clearly it is not simply who is in the family that is important.

The *attitude* of those filling a role is more important than *who* fills it. If a family consists only of women, for instance, is it because the family is patterned or "rigged out" this way—a result of the mother's intolerance of men—or is it an accident of fate? Both kinds of mothers may fulfill a "fathering" role. With one, the family structure is a consequence of an emotional conflict, and this would have its effect on men in the family. With the other situation, where it is an accident of fate, it is likely to be a transient state, and there is probably a "good enough" family structure for the children growing up in the family. What is inside the mother concerning men is more important than whether there is a man in the house. It is the entire family system inside and out, the adaptability of the family in the performance of daily tasks and activities that will determine development. There must be mothering and fathering as well as a sense of what it means to be male and female. The family usually includes adult individuals of different sexes. It *requires* in the minds of all some idea of what it means to be one sex or the other. There must be a clear definition of authority so that the child can progress toward autonomy without losing a sense of safety.

Ideally, in the nurturing, protected, and controlled environment the child interacts intensively with one or another family member in the most precisely determined way, requiring specific kinds of involvement or noninvolvement from other family members during each successive phase. This is not to say that there is *one* correct way to allow a child to grow and develop, or that each minute or day is crucial. Development proceeds by phases, however, and the sum total of growth that the child achieves will depend in very important ways upon the influence of his family. In short, there is a range of helpful responsiveness, and when the family around the child is structured reasonably well, parents usually do at least as well as their own parents did for them.

Children need secure, committed parents, for whom the child's welfare is tied in to their own, parents who have the desire and opportunity to protect their children and to blossom with them. Parents should minimize separations from very young children, and they should minimize envelopment or smothering of them as well. They should learn to grow with their children by growing themselves, through their own self-acceptance, their work, and their continued contact with their growing families of origin. They should learn what to expect, and what is right or wrong about their own family structure with its shifting subsystems, so that they know when and *how* to become involved with a child and when to leave him alone (or with someone else). They can learn these skills from others in a community that functions as a community, as well as from their families of origin. And they should get help from a society that respects the family unit. The family not only structures development, it is our emotional matrix as we live our lives day by day.

Our emotions affect us in many ways. They affect, at any given moment, our sense of well-being, our choices big and small, our marriages, our relationships, work, and pleasures. Like the heart and the kidney, our emotional functioning never stops. Sometimes we are more comfortable than at other times, and sometimes we have difficulties with our emotions. Our problems come from two directions: from inside ourselves, as a reaction to death, separation, marriage, pregnancy, or an illness; or from outside—a disaster or an accident or an economic depression. We often do not perceive these events, however, as causes of our problems. We perceive them frequently as ways in which we fail or ways in which our families fail us. Someone does not behave properly, or we are no longer in love or loved by another. We feel pain. We blame family members around us, and we attack the family as an institution. We decide we should not trust relationships.

Our shortsightedness can have many ramifications. There are emotional, medical, social, and economic consequences to having dysfunctional relationships; the problem can be too much distance, too much closeness, or, most commonly of all, too much rigidity.

Emotional health and vulnerability can be seen in terms of susceptibility at certain growth stages, epidemics of certain kinds of malfunction where some people have a mild case and others are more seriously or permanently stricken.

This is because human growth and development are best understood as a series of continuous separations of body, mind, emotions, and physical presence. The stages themselves are well known: birth, psychological separation at one to two years of age, school, adolescence, marriage, loss of our parents when we marry, loss of our children when they marry, loss of vital functions, and death. As each stage brings a new sense of awareness, the individual behaves differently and there is a shift in the family structure; closeness in one place creates distance somewhere else. The family is rigged out differently at each stage. For instance, infants are close to their mothers or mothering figures, while they are more distant from their fathers. Adolescent boys are close to their fathers and often consider their mothers bothersome. Understanding everyday preferences, attitudes, and behavior as a reflection of this rigging, and the distances of members from each other (which change over time), the changing relationships of the subsystems in the family can be crucial in daily living. It prevents developments, which are really inevitable, from being misunderstood and becoming a source of pain. Knowing that each subunit of the family functions differently from the family as a whole, knowing that the children act up in very specific ways when Father is not there, knowing that family events are just not *felt* in the same way when Mother is not there can eliminate the sense of disappointment in change. Individuals can then endure shifting winds, even storms, in family living and learn what adjustments are likely to be helpful in different situations. Knowing that changes produce other changes, that separations produce other separations, is the first step toward discovering which secondary changes are helpful and which ones add misery to novelty. It is important to know the specific experiences of the life course; and to keep one's emphasis on the self: one's own expectations, disappointments, and knowing and controlling one's automatic reactions in order to expedite creative change in the family system.

In systems terms, growth is a process, while change is an event. Growth is a becoming, change is a new reality. All growth is change, but change may not be growth. Growth is a gradual process. We conceptualize it as being stepwise because it is easier for us to think about it that way. Growth is a series of adaptations to loss of various kinds.

In dealing with loss we do various things, most of them automatically. We feel guilty because we are angry at the loss and at the powerlessness we feel at the passing of time or the randomness of events. After we feel guilty, we blame: "If only I did this . . ." becomes "Why didn't he or she do that . . . ?" Each person in a family is acutely aware of others and only one person decompensates at a time. Yet each should have time to work feelings through and adjust to a new role and a new identity.

When we lose someone or something there is a natural healing process that goes on inside the self. We hold on, we mourn, or we incorporate. We look for parts or aspects or activities, places, attitudes, or feelings of the lost object or person. We do what he did, go where he went, have moods that he had. For instance, when babies who have been raised by depressed mothers are separated from these mothers, they seem to attach themselves and find comfort in the depressed state. (As adults, depressing music can help us feel better when we are sad.)

There is a constant reverberation in the life cycle between attachment and detachment, intimacy and autonomy, security and freedom, from the earliest phases of separation from the mother through all the later stages. We get sick or well, anxious or depressed, poor or rich, all in the service of adjusting our connections, our synapses, with others. We are constrained, protected, and supported by our families. Others close to us influence whatever we do. They exert pulls on us that we are hardly aware of. Some of us feel like satellites revolving around others, unconscious of our linear motion in space. Others of us act like shooting stars, unaware of our rotation around our own axis. Yet we all affect and are affected by each other.

As Dr. James Lynch points out, loneliness makes us more vulnerable to death. Separation increases the risk of heart "failure" in susceptible patients. Stress decreases coronary arterial blood flow and circulation. Physical comforting probably increases it. All these changes are most likely mediated through hormones in the bloodstream, our internal milieu.

Too much closeness is no good either. Failure of psychological separation between family members, too much intrusiveness in thoughts, feelings, controls, and responsibility is probably one of the precursors to psychosomatic disease, like ulcerative colitis or bronchial asthma. The trick seems to be to maintain autonomy without becoming isolated from others or, as Dr. Bowen puts it, to stay in contact without becoming emotionally "entangled."

When there is a problem we feel the strain in the family structure in the two axes relating to sex and generation. We blame the man or the woman; the adults criticize the children, the children "rebel" against their parents, all in response to a natural or unnatural change that must be dealt with. And we can handle problems by shoring up one or another side of the family ship, allowing more flexibility and a better adaptation. Therapists do this in many ways. They help men to ask for love and to cry when they need to. They encourage women, when they are reluctant, to become independent and autonomous and happy with themselves. They encourage parents to give young people authority and freedom, helping them find ways to overcome the fear and loneliness that replace adolescent power struggles when their children become fully adult. And they help mature people find pleasure, excitement, and even sexuality in their older years.

At other times in chaotic families, instead of loosening the structure they clarify and reinforce it. They can create a "generation gap," support authority in parents and sometimes even submission or rebellion in children. They may encourage people to accept masculinity and femininity, men working and women caring for children. We ourselves can also learn to cope with change, in ourselves and in our society through our families. We can learn how families operate in general; then we can know the strengths and weaknesses of our particular family ship and how and why we as individuals came to be on it. I believe we must also go back to know and understand the families before us, our "invisible loyalties," as family therapists Dr. Ivan Bosyormenyi-Nagy and Geraldine Spark put it. Then we can return to our current families with a new awareness and with the strength to use it.

When we become experts on ourselves by knowing our families and how they created us, we can deal with loss or growth through our identifications. We can work through changes as we need to, with people in our families and in the world around us. We can maintain our emotional balance while adjusting to growth and change, and help others in our families maintain theirs.

VI

—— ◇ ——

HOW THE MODERN
FAMILY EVOLVED

THROUGHOUT OUR HISTORY, family adaptations not only varied with the times, they became genetically programmed into individual family members and are part of the biological heritage of modern men and women. As primitive men hunted for survival, those who learned to cooperate in the hunt and live in groups adapted better than those who did not. As in any group, patterns of relationships between members increased in complexity as time went on. The groups became more and more cohesive, and roles more and more specialized. Some people were leaders, some followers, and most performed according to their talents. These patterns must have varied from group to group and era to era.

There was also specialization of roles within the family. Men and women, emerging from a togetherness that was based on sexual pleasure, developed two different roles and an intimate partnership. These family role specializations came from biological imperatives, such as the female's capability for pregnancy and suckling the young, and the male's incapability for childbearing as well as perhaps his physical strength. Other tasks were shared or divided, were frequently interchangeable (male and female were always adjectives, as Virginia Satir points out, not nouns, sharing more common features as human beings than differences), but for the most part, task specialization had to do with the women being with the children close to home and the men being outside. Trust and attachment, unity with diversification, provided the best framework for survival.

The development of male and female roles paralleled the evolution of the family in society. The primordial human condition, even embryologically, is that of the female. The male differentiates because of his gonadal hormones from a femalelike state early in embryonic development. Civilization went from matriarchy to patriarchy with an increasingly complex relationship at home between the man and the woman, no longer limited to sexual functioning, and an increasing cooperation and involvement between peers outside.

Fatherhood, it seems, followed long after motherhood in its development and presupposed a relationship between man and woman, and a society to which both belong. There were "paternal" values—rules and roles related to society that were collective, flexible, and adaptive to the needs of the time and place—and "maternal" values, which were more enduring. Marriage, for instance, is a paternal institution (for both men and women) while parenthood is a maternal one (also for both sexes).

With agriculture and animal husbandry, there was the development of the concept of property, a sense of place, and with harvesting and the knowledge of nature's life cycle, a sense of time. There was more and more specialization for individual men and women. There were healers and midwives, and finally, when there were priests and historians, civilization was born.

We can understand various features of human growth, development, emotionality, and social relationships in the context of our evolution. Most people with mature sexual equipment can have children; only those capable of intimacy and partnership could raise them. Those children who were attached to parents, who invited some reciprocal feelings from a mother figure, had the best chance for survival. We can understand why infants cry when left alone, why they are comforted by a presence, why some who are poor eaters eat well in the company of adults, and why they cry when going to bed as if there were some danger in separation. There was a time when this protest against separation had a real importance, when there really *was* a danger in being left alone.

The security inside the family was built on a continuing emotional relationship between mother and father, and allowed children to master the challenge of separation slowly. They developed a highly complex autonomy during childhood. There could be a prolonged education for survival tasks, and these tasks could be more sophisticated than in other social animals, like the higher primates. Besides the need to overcome separation anxiety, another striking feature of family life in the group was, and is, the incest taboo. Learning control of sexuality in the family encouraged more aggression and coping ability outside it, and allowed for sexual release in adulthood in an intimate emotional relationship with someone outside the family.

Civilized man occupied a very short time in the history of evolution, and we can understand human biology, instincts, and adaptation more in terms of prehistoric than civilized environments. The bodies and families that house us, even as we sit in our suburban homes, our farms, or our apartments, were designed for efficient functioning as part of a hunting or gathering group. Our vacation runs to the sun, or to the ski slopes; the flight to rural areas and to parks and shorelines in our cities are all a reflection of our comfort with a life that has mobility, and a life style that resonates with nature.

In most societies the family provided four things: economic survival, sexual gratification, reproduction, and education. Families differed in time and place as to whether they were matriarchal or patriarchal, isolated or caught up in an interconnected family system. Families have been nuclear or "extended" with active relationships existing on three generational levels—grandparents, parents, and children. Sometimes they have been "extended horizontally" with kinships as the base for economic or emotional activity. They have been monogamous or polygynous, i.e., where one man or woman is the spouse and parent in more than one nuclear family, a phenomenon not unknown to our divorce-prone modern American society.

Regardless of these "variations on the theme," the nuclear family with man, woman, and immature children as a separate unit is universal in over 250 cultures that have been studied by anthropologists.

SOCIOLOGY HAS ALSO contributed to our understanding of the family. Earlier in this century Carle Zimmerman developed a theory of cyclical social change in which families evolve over the course of the great civilizations from "trustee" to "domestic" to "atomistic." The definition refers to how much power there is in the family as compared to the individual, and how much obligation each citizen feels toward others. In the trustee family, living members are guardians of the family name, or property or heritage, and the family has great power over its members, requiring sacrifice of individual goals for the welfare of the family group. Later, in the domestic family, social institutions like government and religion emerge from a group of such families. They take over functions of the family and correct abuses of power that are present in the authoritarian, rigid trustee family structure. In the next style, the atomistic family, power and control over people are minimal, and the government becomes an organization of individuals, its chief function being to help them meet their needs of the moment. People are separate. Relationship is felt to be a burden, and there is a high level of hedonism, divorce, delinquency, illegitimacy, and childlessness in society. Each of these family styles helps the society master its challenges, but each has a certain vulnerability and evolves into the next kind of family structure in cyclical fashion.

William F. Ogburn developed a "progressivist" theory and emphasized how the family is a passive institution which adapts to changes in society at large. These include technological or "material" changes and cultural "nonmaterial" changes. There is a "culture lag" (as described in Alvin Toffler's *Future Shock*) as we adjust first to scientific progress, change our activities, and then incorporate new developments into our attitudes and value system. For instance, as mentioned earlier, with contraception and treatment for venereal disease, sexual intercourse became less dangerous, people became more active sexually, and only then did our moral code and value system change. Nowadays automobiles, consumer appliances in the home, and other developments all function to separate family members who spend more time with friends and less with one another. They come to value individualism and freedom highly.

This theory provides many insights into family life today. As we "progress," society takes over many of the functions of the family, which include economic, educational, religious, and protective functions. In our society, only the emotional function, providing a place for child rearing and for emotional "refueling" for adults, has not been taken over by government agencies. Social agencies, incidentally, are not better at meeting our needs than families. They are simply more efficient (supposedly so) in a large society. And disorganization in our new "defunctionalized" families is reflected in divorce, delinquency, and desertion.

People who live in modern families have an opportunity to focus in a more specific way on the one remaining function: providing emotional satisfaction in relationships. The recent human potential movement—including marriage encounters, sex therapy, and Parent-Effectiveness-Training—are all a reflection of this new focused family. Working on relationships can be most helpful for people who want to improve the quality of their lives. One thought, however, is discomforting. In "The Healthy Family" we saw that the most general characteristic of disturbed families is that members spend all their time and energy working and reworking their relationships with one another, unable to accomplish tasks at hand, while adaptive families can do what they set out to do without the diversion of unfinished emotional family business between members. Our society has created families who spend their time doing what disturbed families do. One can only hope that they retain their potential for doing other things when they are required.

Unlike Zimmerman and Ogburn, who were pessimistic about the institution of the family, Talcott Parsons considered the family transitional rather than disintegrating, still the best framework for living and raising children. His "structure-function" theory had the greatest influence on mental-health workers, probably because he incorporated psychoanalytic understanding in his formulation. In *Family, Socialization and Interaction Process*, written with Robert F. Bales, he saw the family as defunctionalized but also as specialized, or "differentiated," with socialization of children and stabilization of adults as the twofold purpose. He focused on the relationship between the family system and the work system outside, how each affected the other. He defined the post–World War II nuclear family as an open system, isolated from kin and grandparents, a specialized, mobile, self-contained unit, highly adaptive to the demands of industrial society leading to many of the developments mentioned in Chapter 4, "The Family under Fire." Divorce rates are high but divorce is not a problem, only a means of re-forming one's family to adjust better and perform better in one's job or role in society.

Later we shall see how divorce is less benign for children and our future as a society than it is for adults. Traumatic divorces or emotional distance between mother and father in the family of origin are a poor example for normal separation. Children of divorce frequently have problems becoming autonomous as young adults later on. Also, specialization between the sexes can bring isolation of individuals rather than an intimate partnership. The distance between the sexes affects the distance between generations. Husbands and wives are more comfortable being "adults" when they are close and support each other. This is a problem in the one-parent family. Mother (or father) has no one to lean on, or grandparents who do give support are physically vulnerable themselves.

Pushed to an extreme, this drive for efficiency in the new specialized family can create more problems than it solves. The kind of family life it creates is well suited to accomplishing societal tasks like winning world wars or increasing the gross national product. In recent times, however, we have learned that efficiency without human social roots creates fanaticism, instability, and the society's own destruction. Nazi Germany, which tried to replace its families with Aryan breeding farms and concentrations camps, is defunct, while Soviet Russia is these days emphasizing the importance of the family. Ideologies can mobilize us temporarily but cannot sustain us and can never replace families.

We must respect the fact that events over the course of millions of years of evolution have created the human condition. Even the limits of change and choice, the dimensions of flexibility and variation, are the product of worlds and adaptations to them which preceded us. Just as our anatomy is determined by evolutionary forces, so are our relationships and the way we function emotionally. The need for sexual gratification and the need for physical security both promote a certain togetherness. The one-to-one relationship between man and woman that creates other human beings and the one-to-one relationship between mother and child that promotes survival are cyclical and self-perpetuating in human evolution. Each leads to the other at some future point in time. Contraception and abortion can only regulate but never eliminate the need for procreation because it is an emotional, not just a physical, need. The one-to-one relationship nurtures the infant and allows him to grow into an adult with a capability and desire for other new one-to-one relationships for his own adult needs.

The intense, dynamic nature of the bond between two people is unidimensional and rigid. It has a fixed distance, and a generally fixed time span. Yet it is potentially unstable and brings out rational forces. It leads to "triangling," the involvement of a third person—a parent, a child, a therapist, an in-law—who acts as a stabilizing force, liberating the two individuals, giving them new options on the involvement and distance they wish to maintain from others in the threesome. It is on this mixture of geometry, psychology, and biology that all human society rests.

As each member of the triangle is allowed distance, he or she can become different according to age and sex-related functions, joining with other three-member groups to form a small society. Psychoanalytically, one uses different words to describe the same phenomenon. In the Oedipal triangle, the love and wish for exclusive possession of one parent gets repressed, and the identification with the other parent that takes place makes us social beings.

There is in adult life the transient pleasure in sex and the longer-term pleasure for the mother to enjoy closeness with her infant, based on her own infantile experience of being nurtured. Finally, there is the even longer-term emotional comfort and stability derived from parents' identification with their offspring, re-experiencing old dreams, solving old psychological problems, relived through their children.

All of these human needs are probably best provided for within a family framework. This does not mean, obviously, that such pleasures are limited to families. There is tremendous variation in what different people need and what they can handle in sex, intimacy, and stability. There is great variation in what any one individual needs or wants, according to his stage of life and what options the world offers him. It does mean, however, that within flexible parameters, human beings are built to function well within family frameworks and that societies flourish when most of their people spend a good part of their lives, especially their early lives, inside a family.

Parsons points out that the family is still the foundation of society, and that in a complex civilization, social solidarity comes from family solidarity early in development. It is based upon a sense of trust in early relationships that becomes generalized later in obligations and expectations on other axes—economic, political and moral. Trust comes from an acceptance of one's sense of belonging, and it is a currency, an "asset" coined in one's family of origin and stored in one's family of procreation. The family experience is necessary for commitment to others, for availability for the emotional and physical satisfactions of a relationship, and for realizing the potential of a union with someone else. Trust allows people to welcome marriage and its possibilities, like parenthood, as an opportunity to create something that is greater than the two individuals themselves—eventually, for instance, preferring marriage to merely living together.

What is important is not just the capacity for trust, but the vicissitudes of trust in the growth process and in society. We learn *when* to trust, and *how* to trust; also that trust should be earned, given, and accepted in relationships both in families and in society.

Certain societies are the product of an ideology or of conditions which de-emphasize family life in favor of a common societal goal, as in communist countries early in their history, or in the Israeli kibbutz. Others favor a view of life emphasizing or valuing the individual himself without his family, like ancient or modern hedonistic societies or even slave societies. Yet when ideology comes first, families resist change. In the Israeli kibbutz, young adults are choosing in increasing numbers to raise their own children, mother staying at home while father goes off to work. The sharp differentiation in sexual roles, even stereotyping, is seen as a luxury, the gratification of childhood dreams.

The Soviet government, in spite of an early push against the family, viewing it as a self-perpetuating mechanism for the creation of the bourgeoisie, has more recently been vocal in its support of the family, encouraging women, where possible, to raise their own children, de-emphasizing divorce and emphasizing prerogatives for the family unit. Herbert Gutman points out that throughout the history of the South, blacks had monogamous relationships wherever possible and strong family structures with roots in West African kinship patterns. They had a clear image of the family life that was proper and desirable even if it did not exist in their current reality. The black family survived centuries of subjugation, disruption, forced separations, and intermarriage without a government that recognized it, or laws of any kind, state or federal, concerning marriages and domestic family life, that would protect it. The proverbial matriachal black family of modern times, which lacks a male authority figure because father is absent or peripheral, is a product of urbanization, Northern migration and perhaps aspects of a social service system that seems to replace, but often undermines, family cohesion.

A person's need for his family—that primary emotional commitment and the intimacy with others of a different sex and age— always outlasts interference from those who try to bend the family and force it to react to "larger" needs.

If many of the original family functions are now performed by society and its agencies in schools, churches, hospitals, and other organizations, why then is the nuclear family still the most widespread form of living arrangement? Because the other functions, the more basic ones (providing a place conducive to emotional well-being of adult members and protection for the growth and development of the children), have always been the most important ones out of which all the others are derived. The family has always been the most adaptive institution for intimacy and child rearing. It provides a framework for a long-standing, mutually gratifying sexual and emotional relationship, and this is what most people want. The overwhelming majority of people with infant experience in a household with a father and mother identify with one and develop wishes to possess the other. Those with variations on this early experience shape their relationships later in life according to their needs, but the closer they come to having a deep intimate relationship, the more comfortable and functional they are.

Furthermore, parenthood stabilizes and gratifies adults as it nurtures children. Beyond the natural pleasure of raising a child and watching him grow (that strange mixture of identification and separateness), parents are allowed to re-experience needs and feelings from stages of their own development that exist, as Parsons says, as "residua" in their personalities as adults. These early wishes of parents are not simply gratified. The new status as a parent provides opportunity for overcoming emotional conflicts that have limited the individual's functioning since childhood. For instance, men and women who never were allowed certain pleasures or allowed to really be children can relive their childhood by experiencing their children's pleasure. Other patterns include parents who might have enjoyed the pleasures of childhood too much and never gave up certain early wishes until their own children required them to be adults. Seeing a child develop, becoming an increasingly autonomous part of the parent's self and then separating from the parent, stirs these inner conflicts. The disturbing emotions that mothers and fathers feel are sometimes more a result of this rekindling process than of events and real requirements of the child. But if these conflicts are recycled, parenthood can bring a new cohesion to the personality and a new capacity for an enhanced relationship between spouses. A mother who falls apart at her child's first fever, and a father who explodes at his son's willfulness, or parents who are uncomfortable or even resentful toward their child's emerging masculinity or femininity, have motivation, in the form of a child whom they love and identify with, to surpass their old conflicts. Parents have a new opportunity for growth themselves.

The family provides the best environment for growth and development of children, and the reasons behind this have already been explored. In my experience, caring, available, secure parents, involved with each other and with other tasks besides caring for the child, provide the best environment for children to grow into adults with similar capabilities.

VII

TROUBLED-FAMILY
STYLES

FAMILIES CAN BE classified by size, ethnicity, or demography. They describe themselves as black, white, Jewish, Christian, Scandinavian, Mediterranean, "Old South," DAR, or "Hell's Kitchen." All these labels say something about a family, but on a superficial level. Ethnic dimensions have a specificity that matches the costume and the communication style of a family, but ethnic labels tell us only about the "how" and not enough about the "what" of family systems. They tell us more about the color and texture of a family than about its structure, more about what a family looks like than what it is. Besides, most families are blends of characteristics such as urban, rural, first generation, fourth generation, upwardly or downwardly mobile—characteristics which are more important than ethnic ones. Yet people cling to a label as an identification, and usually it is an ethnic one that in the second or third generation becomes more nostalgia and fantasy than reality. We perpetuate these notions by using them not only for identification, especially during times of stress and mobility, but to meet inner psychological needs as well. Some people feel safe marrying "their own kind," while others can relate in a gratifying way and without losing an inner "safety" only to people with a specific ethnic background or stereotype, real or imagined—for instance, Jewish warmth or Irish wit.

The congruence of a family with others in its community or group is also important. If a family is Italian-American, is it more Italian or more American? Does Italian mean Milanese or Sicilian? Norwegians and Danes are both Scandinavian, yet early child-rearing practices and the close mother-child relationship among Norwegians may account, according to Professor Maurice Farber, for a lower suicide rate than among the Danes, who use early child-care services much more routinely.

The most useful classification is one which refers to a family's style of communication and way of perceiving the world (the family boundary) which in turn is a reflection of the way it perceives outsiders and the human condition in general. Do family members worry a lot and fear others in the community? Do they use other families or merge with them (where there is no boundary at all), or do they engage them gradually in the normal course of the individual life cycle? The family can be a citadel where people get together to buy alarm systems, survival foods, and locks for the doors, or it can be a sanitarium where people use their bodies or body orifices to express anger or ask for love. The family can be theater; tragedy, melodrama, or comedy (slapstick or drawing-room). Psychiatrist Helm Stierlin describes families as centrifugal when children are adolescents, spinning them away from a high-energy center. Others are centripetal, attracting them back into the family field whenever they begin to separate. In sum, there are as many ways for classifying families as there are for classifying people.

The following are descriptions of common family patterns which are consistent with adequate functioning for all individual members; yet there is usually a vulnerability which can best be understood in terms of the style of the family's operations. This group of families is distinguishable in its systems characteristics from the families in which the individual is the focus. Families can be a combination of two or more of the styles presented here, and any one of them can produce and at times reinforce problems in a member with severe emotional disturbance. The family structure, however, has greater flexibility and more potential for functioning along the parameters discussed in the description of the healthy family. The particular styles can be understood best as an exaggeration of various specific features of normal and acceptable family structure and function. You may find aspects of yourself or your family in many if not all of these family types. The styles are extreme variations of particular family adaptations, and are simplified for the purpose of presentation. Some of these categories have been described by Drs. Ernest Andrews, Frederick Ford, and Joan Herrick. Most families have qualities of one or more of these types, and all families retain the possibility for growth, change, or adjustment.

CHILDREN COME FIRST

IN A "CHILDREN COME FIRST" family the healthy nurturing function, usually of one parent, is exaggerated. Parents in these families say things like "Don't do it for me, dear, do it for your son [daughter]." The arrival of the young prince or princess in such a family is the fulfillment of a childhood dream in one or both of the parents to take care of baby better than their own parents took care of them. They are determined that things will be set up right this time. No mean older brothers, jealous older sisters, extraneous aunts and uncles. Usually one spouse takes over and makes the other an assistant in the new twenty-four-hour-a-day family job. No more husband and wife, it is caretaker and associate, members of the court for the new crown prince or princess. The chief caretaker has a proven fertility and a new status among friends and relatives. He or she also has a twenty-four-hour-a-day companion, a new resource, a new power, and hope for the future. The wish to "re-do" things right and protect this new companion against loss or pain of any kind inhibits the baby's growth. It is an "I'll show you" message to the particular parent's family of origin, in this case, "I'll show you how to be a mommy [or a daddy]." Sometimes the message is a fantasy in the mind of the parent. Sometimes the family of the new baby becomes a center of attention and the message is delivered on a regular basis to actual family members, grandparents, aunts and uncles of the new infant. It can be mother or father who has this dream and or wish. Mother can watch her baby twenty-four hours a day and tell father to "eat at the diner." Father can come home early for the first time in his marriage, give Mother a peck on the cheek and say, "Now where's Daddy's sweetheart?" or "Where's the champ?" This superparent is protecting the infant against the events and feelings that occurred during his or her own childhood, and in the very act of protectiveness, can cause history to repeat itself. A woman whose father left the family when she was a child can be so concerned about protecting her own baby from a similar fate that she ignores her husband, who leaves the marriage in disgust. A man whose mother died when he was a child can "mother" and protect his new baby and ignore his wife, who will resent the baby and desert both husband and child emotionally. Behavior in families implies expectations of others which can become self-fulfilling prophecies. There is a new separateness between parents in the "children come first" family. There is freedom to ignore or instruct the spouse, to tell him (or her) how inadequate or inconsiderate he (or she) is in caring for or loving the child. Daddy sometimes takes a back seat right out of the marriage, especially when this pattern is combined with the "Male as Drone" type of family. Mother can become depressed, feel superfluous and helpless to enter the new loving twosome between Daddy and his little girl or his new pal. To do their duty, children try to remain as infantile as possible, for as long as possible. Spouses also learn that when they really want something, they must behave like a child to get it. In its extreme form, this kind of family creates vulnerability, with one parent depressed and the other more and more peripheral to the real goings on in the family; there is a chaotic family structure. Children remain infants emotionally, with poor tolerance for frustration, for siblings, for schoolmates, or for increasing responsibility. They develop a life-long desire to remain the infant.

Whichever spouse is overinvolved in this way uses parenthood to withdraw from life. He or she is intolerant of people, unable to give and take and negotiate with others. Such parents give up on other adults whom they dislike and devote themselves to their children, whom they can control. At first the children are dependent because they are small; later they are dependent because they feel so guilty and inadequate. Everyone in the family calls it love because these parents use language any way they please. It is really a possessiveness and a need for control to burden the child with guilt, keeping him forever imprisoned, so that he dreams of the day when he can have children of his own to live for and sacrifice for and control. These families resemble the martyrdom-type families. Each generation exists for and surrounds the lives of its children, and the families resemble the Russian dolls within the dolls within the dolls.

The appropriate solutions to the problems of living with this kind of family pattern are to be found in a new self-awareness and self-esteem in the caretaking parent, and in a new supportive relationship between husband and wife where each appreciates the other's role and participates in it. They then have less need to use the children to derogate and control their spouse. They need time without the children, to be by themselves, to find a deep awareness of their own place in their own family of origin. One must know one's own tendencies and sore points, and combine this knowledge with good communication with one's spouse. The children can then be raised by the parental unit and not by mother or a father alone, each doing less than half the job.

"TWO AGAINST THE WORLD"
("IT'S THEM AGAINST US")

THIS KIND OF FAMILY is based on a relationship between two people who share their distrust of outsiders. Children are accepted until they grow up and want to bring friends home or want to marry, or voice ideas from "out there" that only serve to confuse Mother and Dad who decided all there was to decide years before. Children eventually are either extruded or cut off from such a family or remain within the family, usually without, but sometimes with, a temporary or permanent mate. This mate is never to be trusted, regardless of how similar his views are to those of the family of origin. Things that reduce the danger from "out there" upset the relationship between husband and wife who do all things together. There is little time spent between any one particular parent and one or another child. Aunts and uncles, like the children, one at a time, eventually become outsiders too. When the children grow up, the cutoff from school, church, and community can be complete, and Mother and Dad seldom go out. Children come to them. And as time goes on, sometimes their behavior, thinking, and view of things can even be at odds with reality.

SWEETIE AND SNOOKIE

SWEETIE AND SNOOKIE have another kind of "togetherness" marriage. They never call each other by name but treat each other as the infants they are throughout their lives, not just in the bedroom or at home, but everywhere. They ask and require that all others in and out of the family call them by their pet names and accept them as infants in a fixed role. Bound together symbiotically, often since adolescence, husband and wife fill each other's needs and are together as much as possible. One partner is usually aggressive and dominant, the other passive, so much so that there is a marked sexual skew to the family. Symbiosis becomes a pattern for parasitism and there is little social conscience outside the family. Self-centered, they relate to all others, including children and family members, only in terms of what they can get for themselves. They have children for the purpose of being entertained by them and supplied in their emotional needs. As can be expected, the children function poorly and are chronically angry or depressed. Tragedy is replete in these families, and if a child dies, there is little mourning for him or her. Sweetie uses the youngster's room for her needlepoint or Snookie takes it for his model cars or helmets. They blame others and are angry rather than sad over loss and remain so for only a short period of time. They function poorly outside the home. Snookie works only so Sweetie can buy what she wants.

The more exaggerated the domination and submission, and the more inappropriate the relationship, the more secure they feel about each other, since no one else would ever tolerate such behavior. There is little love or achievement in these families, little compassion and no morality, only more or less anger and unhappy children. It is really a "children come last" type of family. As hangers-on to a larger group they can function reasonably well, but when they have children the results can be tragic. Children, youngsters particularly, need support from friends, relatives, and therapists in this kind of family. After they have grown and leave the household, life for Sweetie and Snookie can be stable just as long as they remain together.

EVERY MAN FOR HIMSELF

HUSBAND AND WIFE in this kind of relationship create a family where members are partners in a common quest; wealth, objects, status, attractiveness, intellectual or athletic achievements, represent the "Golden Fleece." Members have no other real bond between them. They can be friendly, cooperative, or uninterested in the others in the family except insofar as the particular goal, whatever it may be, is concerned. There is little intimacy, warmth, or family feeling, and members communicate only to keep score, attack one another or judge one another's performance. Although there is a fairly constant threat of separation in the quest for success, members do not help those who are in pain or who need support because they cannot ask one another for help. Faced with problems, the family splits apart—unlike other families, which pull together. Children growing up in this kind of atmosphere develop peculiar value systems because feedback between family members is inconsistent and convoluted. Children are distant yet never really separate or capable of intimacy outside the family any more than inside it. Communication reflects the sameness of goals and the lack of interest in people as people.

There are few questions, answers, or exchanges, while there are many judgments, provocations and surprise responses. Families with some of these characteristics can sometimes grow when they realize that their value system doesn't bring them the happiness they desired. Sometimes with family therapy they can learn to communicate more openly and feel more deeply about one another, especially if one member with a strong feeling for someone else in the family uses a kind of emotional domino theory which eventually touches all members. They can sometimes find what they are looking for, perhaps closer to home than they thought.

MUTUAL TORTURE
(OR *WHO'S AFRAID OF VIRGINIA WOLF?*
TYPE FAMILIES)

THIS IS ANOTHER type of "togetherness" family with little room for children or other outsiders, where mates are locked into each other through hate. The dictionary meaning of "torture" is not only "to inflict pain," but to distort, as in to "torture" the meaning of a sentence. The dedication, concentration, and endurance of the rage and torment of these couples is due to the "torturing" or distortion of the image each creates of the other and for the other in order to stay connected through anger. Their rage is an eternal fire that sometimes smolders and sometimes blazes. Their life is a constant testing, provocating, with fixed rules as to how far each can go, and frequent threats to break the rules. Suggestions of separation, other interests for either partner, are inevitably resented. Life is one long argument, with doors slammed, only to be opened and slammed again in a hollow gesture of threatened separation. They drink too much, to punish each other, and take drugs to create emergencies requiring the other to attend to them and take care of them. There are fixed roles or they alternate parts.

Sometimes this kind of interaction is a temporary state prior to separation. At other times such couples grow old hating, needing, and caring for each other. When things go awry, it is because one member breaks down or because someone or something outside their interaction interferes. Complaints about the partner are usually an attempt to engage and frustrate the listener, whether it is a child, an in-law or a therapist. For those who wish some measure of change, conjoint therapy can be useful in decreasing some of the anger. Without conflict, however, depression and loneliness erupt in one or both partners. But the experience of depression, an increased tolerance for it, and an understanding of its origin can be helpful for these individuals.

I NEED LOVE/I NEED REST

THIS IS THE KIND of family that psychiatrist Peter Martin describes as "the lovesick wife and the coldsick husband," also known clinically as the "hysterical wife and the obsessive husband." In this kind of marriage one spouse, usually the woman, is unhappy and depressed and may even have physical complaints because she feels unloved. Her husband is not passionate or attentive or tender enough to meet her needs. He is cold or cruel or "always tired," just not interested in saying or doing things that will make her feel loved. Sometimes she suspects there is something wrong with her, that she is insatiable. Her husband sometimes says or hints that he thinks so. At other times, in a different mood, she might suspect that her husband just does not like women. She is unhappy in the marriage, wants this love from her husband, not from someone else, and it seems he will not or cannot give it. "If only he would change." Sometimes the woman leaves her husband, marries a passionate lover, only to find the same situation in a second, third, or fourth marriage, or that the lover is unsatisfactory in other ways. Women friends with whom she discusses her feelings sometimes have the same complaints. Activities outside the home do not interest them. These women are resigned, depressed, and depend upon their husbands to relieve their depression.

The husband in such a marriage complains that his wife nags him. His wife needs constant love and attention, and he just cannot give it. He works all day and when he comes home he wants to rest. Angry, afraid of closeness, he wants to be left alone to read or to watch television, in a solitary activity rather than through a relationship. Finally he is manipulated by guilt into doing things with wife and family until, enraged or exhausted, he gets out for a few hours or a few days. Such men are frequently found in taverns, cocktail lounges, or on business trips.

The perceptions and complaints in this type of marriage and

family environment are particularly common and exist to a degree in perhaps most marriages. They are related in part to the differences in development and upbringing between men and women in our society. In early life, some girls learn little more in their families than how to love and be loved. Little boys are encouraged too exclusively to be strong and independent. Little girls begin to feel loved for what they are, while little boys become valued for what they do. Although the psychological needs for development have not changed, child-rearing practices have, and recently, polarization of sex roles is less than it has been in the past. This change may help some of the women in these kinds of families understand that they are not really so dependent on being loved by someone from the outside, as it may help some of the men understand that love, affection, tenderness, and tears are not inappropriate for a man in today's society.

The man usually needs this kind of interaction as much as his wife. The marriage can be stable though conflictual, the spouses comfortable at having each other, yet punishing each other at the same time. Often the relationship is the result of a collusion between a wife who complains about but expects rejection, and a husband who deprecates yet is only really comfortable with dependent women. An effort to work at the marriage, doing different things, experiencing new feeling states, can help these families. With professional help the roots of this kind of discomfort can be explored. There is a type of man who punishes his wife for needing and loving him as he was punished and rejected for needing and loving his parents when he was a boy. There is a type of woman who expects her husband to fulfill the fantasies she had about her father. Again, a certain kind of man avoids his wife the way his father feared and avoided his wife (or perhaps should have avoided his wife, who nagged him in front of the children).

Exploration of earlier relationships and experiences, especially in childhood when spouses learned what girls and boys were supposed to do and what they could expect, can be combined with the couple's own efforts at trying something new and may be helpful with these families. With less rigid sex-role stereotyping, more flexibility in raising children, and healthy communication that goes along with partnership in marriages, younger families of today and families of the future may be spared this kind of inter-action and the pain that goes along with it.

THE MALE AS DRONE

THESE FAMILIES constitute the modern matriarchies. The woman marries on her own terms, stays close to her own parents, some-times in the same building or house or "mother and daughter estate," keeps the husband around as an ornament, a "fly on the wall," usually until the children are born, after which there is a divorce. The woman functions primarily as a mother (similar to the "children come first" type of family) and very little as a wife. If there is remarriage, after another child or two there is a "re-divorce." The real power in the family lies with the mother; that is, the mother and the grown female children. The husband is not to be trusted, is nagged so much about his "affairs" that he usually has them, thus bringing another woman into the family fold. This is the kind of family where a man's first and second wives can become friends, all dealing with him as a subject of conversation, more as an image than as a real person; he is a stud, a recruiter, and collector of women, although according to them, he always remains fragile and undependable. The girls as future mothers are more highly prized than the lonely, rejected, vulnerable boys, who end up looking for a powerful woman to marry later on in life.

LOCKER-ROOM FAMILIES

"LOCKER-ROOM" families idealize boys just as "powder-room" families idealize girls. These homes are filled with baseball bats, boxing gloves, roughhousing, and sudden silences followed by the crash of broken furniture or china. Boys seem more highly valued than girls because they can do things together with father, are chums, and protect each other. As far as the young boys in the family are concerned, girls are a burden. The important thing that is lacking in these families is comfort with sexual identity and capacity for love, esteem and respect for the opposite sex in the parents. The other important features are sibling position and family structure. "Little sisters" are more vulnerable in these kinds of families than "big sisters." When there are a number of boys in the family, and they grow up without close contact with girls, one of the boys may end up being the girl among the boys and may become uncomfortable with his sexual identity. When the adults in the family confirm the view of things that overvalues masculinity, Sister thinks that perhaps it is true that she is not as good or powerful or useful as a boy and she either becomes angry or depressed, or she tries to do what the boys do as well or better than they. It is not the number of men and the activities they perform together that is the most important feature of these "locker-room" families, but the parents' inner feelings about the sexes, their own early experience of learning what it meant to be a little girl or boy themselves, especially as compared to their own brothers and sisters. Despite a powerful vocal group of boys influencing the atmosphere and sexual value system of the family, a mother aware of her needs and comfortable with her own femininity can balance out any number of boys if she functions in a partnership at the head of the family with a father who accepts women.

YOU'RE WRONG, I'M RIGHT

EACH MEMBER of this kind of couple is not interested in torturing the other as much as in proving that he or she is right. To them, being right is the most important thing in the world. Each must prove his or her superiority. The need is a compulsive one and comes from early childhood when there is a vulnerability due to a sense of imperfection or inferiority that is overwhelming. Sometimes it is related to early perceptions about one's sex or sibling position; at other times it is related to a parental figure who seems omnipotent, superhuman, and perfect to the small child. In either case, these children grow up vulnerable and strive for superiority and perfection to overcome it. Frequently they do well in school and socially, and when they become King or Queen of the

Campus they are considered the perfect couple, meant for each other. After a tasteful wedding ceremony, a magnificent reception —the social event of the season—and a delightful honeymoon, they discover that they do not know each other, they merely shared the spotlight. They do not even know how to talk to each other; they merely did the same things at the same time. Never having learned cooperation, they resort to competition. As each waits for expressions of the other's admiration, disappointment turns to rage. The old threat of humiliation, inferiority, and rejection is awakened, and life becomes guerrilla warfare on a twenty-four-hour-a-day basis. Decision making becomes impossible. Children, friends, and family are ignored as each lies in wait for an opening, a slip-up by the other. They bluff, threaten, have temporary truces, allow the other to win because they are "above the fight," thereby taking a moral victory for the time being. Compromise is felt as weakness, giving to the other as defeat. Often these couples are doomed to their unhappy existence. Sometimes, with life experience, therapy, problems to work out or tragedies to work through, they can become aware of giving, feeling sides of themselves, and they can face the helplessness, vulnerability, and low self-esteem that is underneath their competitiveness and see it for what it is—a remnant of the past.

MARTYRDOM

FAMILY MEMBERS here say things like "You go out and have a good time." Added to this is the important ingredient "I don't mind." The real communication beneath the words goes something like this: "I have no wishes or needs. My happiness and my very life depend on you. Do what you will." This denial of feeling and need renders the martyr near-perfect, a permanent asset to the other in a family relationship. Something about them, however, hangs like a weight around the neck of those who are trapped by such ploys, even as they use similar tricks themselves. Known also as the "Jewish Mother Syndrome," although it is no more limited to Jews than is circumcision, martyrdom is related to the constant politeness of "After you, Alphonse," or "Killing them with kindness" type of families.

For those who use it, it is a way of maintaining control and requires a certain kind of guilt sensitivity in others who are thus manipulated. Usually the controller and prey choose each other on the basis of their emotional availability to this kind of inter-action. The controller wants nothing for herself (it is usually the mother in the family), only to make the others happy. In the others' happiness she finds her own. Beneath the altruism and denial of self-identity is a rigidity born of poor self-esteem. Nego-tiation and flexibility are unknown. There is only getting one's way; by deviousness and manipulation, simultaneously denying one's wishes so as not to begin a battle for control. Beneath "Your happiness is my happiness" is "My happiness and security depend upon my control over you," providing an additional example that words are used not as communication, but to accomplish certain goals. Power is retained by the controller and that is the way she likes it because basically she does not trust others and cannot deal with not getting her way.

There are few arguments, only sulking. There is guilt and hurt, but little anger and open communication. The pain of guilt is the worst of all possible worlds for both parties, and they yield to anything to avoid it themselves, trying to inflict it on the other to maintain control. Making another person feel guilty is like having cash in the bank, a permanent credit balance. Sometimes one partner consistently controls the other in this fashion. At other times they alternate roles. The martyr can be a victim of injustice or can desire change in the other for the other's own good, all as long as nobility is maintained. These couples can lock into each other in a constant struggle, which they call devotion, or they can sacrifice and separate, admit guilt, forgive each other, and "kill with kindness," again in a cyclical fashion. Separations are usually temporary and designed to hurt the partner.

Whether it is spouses treating each other this way or parents treating their children, with awareness and expression of feelings of need, hurt, and anger, one can begin to accept oneself. With growth in a marriage and success in some capacity at home as a parent or at work or play, the "martyr" can begin to feel unique, deserving, and desirable, and can then accept his or her human imperfections and fallibility without old fears of disaster. At that point he or she can give in to another family member without giving up; manipulation ends and real communication begins.

YOU'RE KILLING ME

JUST AS THERE are families where members say, "Look what I'm doing for you," there are others where they say, "Look what you're doing to me." In both systems, guilt is the currency of the realm, and control its most desirable commodity. These families are different from those where members have real illnesses (which will be discussed in a later chapter). Here I am referring to families where the possibility or threat of illness is used as a communication. The "sick" or vulnerable member wants control over the availability and loving concern of others, as shown by their ability to be hurt or to worry about the patient. This style exists in families where the founding members were worried over as children, got their parents' or caretaker's attention when sick, and perhaps did not get it otherwise, and developed few other ways of asking for it. Feeling cared about because of someone's concern over one's body dates back to early childhood, even before the capacity for verbal communication develops. Physical symptoms are simply a way of asking for attention. "Look what you're doing to me" (and the variation on the theme, "Look what they're doing to me") is often a last-ditch attempt to get this kind of caring from a family member or stranger, often a doctor or a nurse. Sometimes it is a regular feature of family living; at other times it is a temporary reaction to stress.

The particular vulnerabilities which turn into complaints are frequently those involving life itself: eating, breathing, choking, "my heart," and it almost seems as if the "patient" hangs on by using others around him as a life line. Sometimes the threat to life exists in the fantasies of all concerned. Sometimes the pattern follows a real illness or physical condition which actually has been life-threatening. One particular family member can use this style of communication, or the role can be interchangeable and vary from one person to another, including children. In these families, individuals usually take turns and seldom does it happen that more than one member needs help at a time. Certain preconditions for this type of interaction are necessary. When availability or care are not forthcoming, anger builds up in the patient. He then gets the symptom and "punishes" the rest of the family. At first they seem to expect, invite, and even like the sense of crisis. They feel guilty, perhaps, about their coldness, or they like the closeness of a worried family, a closeness they do not usually allow themselves. The cry is heard, "There she [or he] goes again," family members drop what they are doing and tend to the patient, ignoring other business, so that the family becomes dysfunctional.

Members are either taking care of the patient or running away. Life becomes a series of crises; when one ends another is about to begin. Apathy and anger replace real concern, and the patient becomes a burden. Communication obviously is unclear. People do not know why they are angry and depressed, what they need and how to ask for it. Indeed, the very foundation of the family with a vulnerable spouse choosing someone who communicates in similar fashion, or conversely, someone who is cold and uncommunicative, reveals sometimes a lack of judgment, a poor understanding of what it means to communicate love, hate, fear, and need freely.

Whether family members go on to die, become seriously ill, lead emotional lives of quiet desperation, or learn other ways of communicating their feelings depends upon their individual growth, self-acceptance, and capacity for a new kind of interaction. The family therapy approach is particularly useful with this kind of problem because one family member cannot change without affecting the others. But if one individual in this kind of family can learn to communicate verbally and emotionally, *feel* feelings, and express wishes and responses more openly, others in the family may then take the chance and express their own feelings more directly.

I HATE MY FAMILY

"YOUR FAMILY may be good for you," many people say, "but my family sure isn't good for me. You just don't know my family."

Statements like "My mother is horrible, my father is a drunk"
arouse anxiety in others. They sense something wrong, sometimes
wish to correct the person, commenting, "You don't really mean
that." True as these statements may be, articulating them over
and over is suspect. Perhaps it stirs up feelings in all of us of the
subjectiveness and nonrationality of the way we look at our own
families. One shouldn't look at others in his family in the same
way that one looks at strangers. Yet some people who had problems in their childhood can talk truthfully about family members
in descriptive terms without stirring up discomfort in others.
Their tone is less angry. They have more knowledge, give more
information about the parent as a person in his time or place.
Their comments are less accusatory and their descriptions are
more full and forgiving. They do not seem to be angry and they
are not saying something about themselves. They are talking
about the past without being controlled by it.

There are many people who grew up in a family where they
were unhappy and who are angry about it later on. Their anger
may be justifiable. Their family may have been unhappy or disturbed, but if these individuals still feel the resentment powerfully and frequently in themselves, they are still connected with
their family, regardless of how far away they appear to be. Leaving the family was an amputation which did not heal, rather than
the uncoupling of a separable part. The wounds are open and
there is usually a limitation in some area of living for these
people.

All of us at one time or another get angry and hate each and
every family member. It is an inevitable part of intimate daily
living. Feeling hate or need or attachment persistently toward a
person in particular usually results from failure to see, hear, and
know the family as a whole. Family contact then is a source of pain,
a reminder of old frustrations that are still alive and that still
function to limit relationships in and out of the family. These
individuals wish for vengeance because they still desire the pleasures and fear the punishments of childhood. They fight against
depression. They form relationships and families of their own that
are limited in their functioning, structured to minimize the re-
awakening of old feelings from the family of origin that are so

threatening or depressing or infuriating. Alone yet not independent, sometimes they seek pleasure in drugs, in relationships that they try to keep superficial for fear of awakening painful dependency feelings. Often these new relationships take on a life of their own, becoming a source of real satisfaction as well as anxiety and conflict.

The intensity, depression, and sexual experimentation remind one of adolescence. These people are as ships lost at sea, unable to steer a course. They are at the mercy of the elements. Many people who say they reject their family are still very much a part of it, and the way in which they remain connected limits their current functioning. They give up their family "cold turkey," leaving issues unresolved, and remain perpetual adolescents, angry at their parents but never separate from them. Or they repeat their problems in their new families with their own children.

Work with families of origin is most helpful for people with this kind of limitation of functioning. Everything about a person, including strengths and capacity for pleasures, is a reflection of different aspects of the family as it was. Knowing the specific ways he was and is part of his family allows a person more freedom from the past and less limitation in the present than he gets from straining to distance himself from the scenes of old battles and old pleasures.

VIII

—— ◇ ——

SPECIAL PROBLEMS

CERTAIN FAMILIES go along with and even reinforce specific illnesses, conditions, or life choices of one or more family members
which become self-perpetuating situations. Therefore, it is often
important to focus on individuals as well as on family structures.
Since the family is a dynamic living system with each part simultaneously affecting and affected by other parts in a circular way,
there are no simple linear cause-and-effect relationships between
family type and individual development or activity. Particular constellations, however, frequently go along with particular individual
categories. In a general way it is the interplay between individual
and family that is important. We look to biology and family history
to understand development, but we look to family structure and
feedback mechanisms to determine a person's ability to function in
the present. What does a particular role or behavior do for others
in the family? What triggers a problem and what maintains it?

SCHIZOPHRENIA

SCHIZOPHRENIA is a condition, temporary or permanent, of heightened sensitivity to perceptions, both internal and external.

Schizophrenic people are caught up in their own thinking and are easily overwhelmed by stress. The logical thought processes that are usually taken for granted and that go into decision making—concentration, communication, relationships with others, and even the sense of reality—are impaired. These individuals can appear isolated or inappropriate and often have limitations in one or more areas of their functioning. The disorder can be acute or chronic and can be more or less disabling. Patients can have one episode or occasional episodes and function well in between, or they can be totally incapacitated. The illness can apparently occur at any age, can take many forms, and can usually be controlled all or in part by medication, although sometimes it brings the most intense kind of psychic pain and can, despite all efforts, destroy the patient. It is similar in many ways to epilepsy and diabetes, and certain people seem more susceptible to it than others, but specific episodes are usually traceable to specific kinds of stress. People who have schizophrenia, or a susceptibility to it, are vulnerable to change—social, physical, or domestic change—in the same way that people with diabetes or epilepsy are vulnerable to carbohydrates in their diet or excitability. A person with this condition provides a challenge for those around him, and families usually take on a particular kind of structure, sometimes protecting and supporting the vulnerable member, sometimes aggravating his condition.

Some of the earliest concepts of family process came from work with families who had a schizophrenic member. Schizophrenia was for this new therapy what hysteria was for Freud—an illness the understanding of which provided insights into normal functioning.

These insights included ideas about family structure and communications within the family system. Dr. Murray Bowen described a kind of "fusion" that was especially characteristic of families where schizophrenia occurred. This was a kind of psychological "stuck-togetherness" between individuals in their thoughts and feelings, especially in their ideas about the responsibility they thought they had for each other.

Dr. Theodore Lidz and his co-workers at Yale talked about

family "schism" (chronic irresolvable conflict between family members) and "skew" (power in the family lies not with a strong mother–father alliance but in a coalition between a parent and a child). He observed that the thinking of one or more members could be irrational, that parents could be "impervious" and emotionally uninvolved with their children and their needs, and that sexual and generational boundaries were not clear. One parent might seem childlike, and a child might have the responsibility of an adult. Fathers might appear to "go out on dates" with daughters, while mothers might even share beds with sons. Roles were confused, with father sometimes passive and mothers unaffectionate but dominant. Generation boundaries could be blurred, with father seductive or overly affectionate in too explicit a way with their daughters, mothers the same way with their sons. Healthy separateness between people in their psychological functioning, distance between members, reasonably appropriate expectations of the male and female roles and the adult and child roles, were all lacking.

These structural features seem to go along with a kind of egocentricity in family members, an inability to perceive things in the world as having an independent existence outside themselves and an inability to relate fully in a loving way to one another.

In California Drs. Don Jackson and Jay Haley and anthropologist Gregory Bateson also worked with families where there was a schizophrenic member. They observed the communication between individuals in the family system and defined a certain kind of mixed message as the "double-bind." These were messages that had different meanings, usually opposite ones, on different levels. They are confusing and frustrating, especially for children, and impossible to understand and integrate mentally and emotionally. Perhaps the first double-bind came from Ecumenicus in the sixth century B.C. who said, "I am Cretan," and followed it by saying, "All Cretans are liars." Such a framework naturally has something of an effect on any subsequent communication. Other mixed messages or instructions might be "Kiss your mother" from a mother who pulls away, saying one thing verbally and another nonverbally, or "Be independent" from a domineering parent whose commanding tone undercuts the very content of the message. Understanding a double-bind is like trying to learn a second language in a first language that changes unpredictably.

There are other communication problems in families where there is schizophrenia, such as disqualifications and fragmentation of information. In these cases, communication has no understandable purpose; it is disruptive and unfocused.

Because children learn from their parents, identify and react to their specific attitudes, perceptions, and relationships, those who grow up in families with these kinds of communication patterns, perceive the world as inconsistent, ambiguous, and overwhelming. They fail to develop the capacity to deal with stimuli in an organized way. The ability to focus, to integrate stimuli, to link meaning to thought to language, and communicate it to others, is impeded. These people and their families are sometimes known in their community as eccentric. They sound the wrong way in the wrong places; they behave privately in public and publicly in private. The blurred boundary between the family and society, as evidenced by their eccentricity, is a reflection of the blurred, disordered psychological process in the individual. The members depend fully on one another for self-esteem, feel responsible for one another, control and feel controlled by one another in a total way. They depend on others in the community, friends and agencies, yet they never really join groups outside the family. They run away from their families, yet never really leave them.

Lately, researchers have been less impressed with family behavior as a cause of this condition and more interested in how family operations sustain or are affected by schizophrenic behavior. Also, there has been interest in schizophrenia as a multi-generational phenomenon, the end result of many generations of lack of psychological "differentiation," according to Dr. Bowen, rather than of specific influences in any one generation even in the first few years of life. The millions who suffer with this condition are neither divine, as was once thought, nor uncontrollably deranged, but human like the rest of us. They need stability in their lives, help in controlling anxiety, through medication, stress avoidance, and different expectations, and most of all, they need *support*, from others in the family or outside it, who neither scapegoat nor impose their own wishes or expectations on them.

SUICIDE

PEOPLE COMMIT suicide or attempt it when they feel overwhelmed by a problem situation and have run out of other possible solutions. The situations vary as much as the ways of dying, but the most important aspect of a suicide is the hidden meaning or purpose of the act. Regardless of the immediate history or mental state of the person, or the method and context of the self-destruction, it is always a choice designed to accomplish some purpose understandable in terms of the person's life and family history. Sometimes it is a response to feelings concerning family members of the past, a wish to join parents or siblings who are gone. These people are lonely, isolated, unreachable, and emotionally "dead," even in the midst of family and friends who are, or have been, available and loving, and even if currently exhausted, could become loving again. At other times, suicide is provoked by specific emotional interplay going on in the family. People in an unstable family situation who have heard or felt a parent's rejection of them very early in life can carry the potential for their own destruction with them throughout their lives. Dr. Joseph Richman of the Albert Einstein College of Medicine in the Bronx, New York, has described, in the most thorough and insightful manner, the various kinds of family disturbances that make a suicidal act understandable. When a situation arises where people wish to gain control of others, or get some rest from an impossibly tense situation for themselves or their families, they may attempt suicide. Frequently they do it as a response to a change or a loss of some important relationship; at other times it is a reaction to failure of efforts to grow and move away from the family. It can be a way of getting out of the house and family, or back into it after being kicked out! Finally, it can be used to maintain a certain status quo. Along with any of these motivations, it can be an attempt to call attention to a disturbed situation which has gone on for years but suddenly becomes intolerable. Wise professionals learn to deal with these complex motivations. Family members around a suicidal patient can have feelings they are entirely unaware of, to punish or be rid of such a difficult person. Sometimes they can remove him from a hospital against medical advice, can leave weapons or drugs around the house, and even drop hints about their dreaded fears and expectations. A suicidal patient feels a sense of failure at meeting his obligations, and he feels angry at family members who cannot help him solve his problems. Yet the communication patterns of these families in this kind of crisis are markedly disturbed, especially regarding expressions of anger. The person most inhibited in this regard, for whom it is most forbidden to express anger, is the suicidal patient himself. He is a family scapegoat, the guilty party, and the "crime" varies with the family. Sometimes he is the dependent one, sometimes the sexual (or homosexual) one, and most often the angry one. In most cases, suicidal impulses are temporary, and the acute situation can be understood in terms of family events and can often be resolved with family emotional resources.

DEPRESSION

DEPRESSION IS A STATE of mind known to all human beings and is characterized by a feeling of helplessness, often accompanied by a sense of sadness. There is a feeling that one is unable to perform or be pleased, and there are changes in one's bodily functions. The diagnostic manual that psychiatrists and other mental health professionals use lists five different categories of depression. There are few kinds of human functioning where the interplay between mind, body, and events outside are so clearly interrelated.

The most important distinction between the different types of depressive illnesses is whether the condition is caused or accompanied by changes in the body's neurochemistry. Certain people have cyclical changes in their neurophysiology and are susceptible to deep depressions that affect them physically. With prolonged depressive feelings, there is a slowing down of bodily functions. Organ systems with smooth muscle tissue are the most dramatically affected by this "slowing." Bowel function slows and the person becomes constipated. Uterine functions are retarded and women stop menstruating regularly. Blood pressure and libido are low and people have no energy or sex drive. There is insomnia, difficulty falling asleep, and especially, early-morning awakening. Many people develop poor appetite and lose weight. For people with this kind of susceptibility, depressions are not related to loss or change in the world outside, but to the changes within themselves. This kind of predisposition can run in families, especially from the maternal side, and cause depression that is marked by these physical signs. It is very common for these individuals to wake up spontaneously at four, five or six o'clock in the morning, in a tense, agitated, or immobile state, sometimes in a sweat, unable to fall back to sleep. The body's diurnal rhythm seems to be malfunctioning. Depressions of this kind, along with manic-depressive disorders, are the kinds of conditions that respond best to medication. Wherever there is a depression severe enough to be accompanied by or caused by these physical changes in the body's functioning, medication can help.

Many families in which one or more individuals are depressed have a value system that emphasizes achievements. Parents, for instance, can be very involved in the performance of their children in the social as well as the intellectual or athletic arenas. Willy Loman in Arthur Miller's *Death of a Salesman* was highly invested in his son Biff's popularity and athletic prowess, depending on him to gain the power and success and acceptance that Willy himself always craved.

Children whose parents depend on them in this way grow up feeling that they are lovable and worthwhile only in proportion to their performance and achievements. If they lose their parents' love when they are not superior, they begin to hate themselves when they fail to do well later on, and carry this attitude with them all their lives. These families can be isolated from others around them, different in some way in racial, religious, or economic status from families in the neighborhood. Often there is an unusual or dramatic family history, a tragedy, a loss of status or money, or a family member with mental illness. The person depressed is frequently the family's hope for regaining prestige. The families can be cold emotionally, authoritarian, often with a strong mother and a weak, absent, or perhaps emotionally unavailable father figure. The future depressive is competitive, conventional, conscientious, successful, and intolerant of his own feelings, especially anger, dependency, or rebellious feelings. Performance is all that counts. Success is survival, and feelings or relationships for their own sake are secondary and pushed aside.

In the early history of many depressed people, there is the loss of a parent. In trying to cope and make sense of a loss, a child gets depressed, worried and guilty, and his self-esteem is affected. Another mechanism is when a mother or father is depressed and a child feels the *emotional* loss of the parent, and in identifying with such a parent, gets a grim view of the world.

People in these families are strongly bound to one another, not so much in showing their love but in doing things for one another, denying anger and the wish to be separate, always working hard to make one another proud. They have the most trouble saying openly that they need the others. One parent can be the driving force, with the family focused around him or her, children finding their places according to their genetic make-up and their family-designated role. Through research and new understanding, we now know that unrecognized depression was probably the force in many families behind alcoholism, suicide and tragedies; it can also run side by side with driving ambition, great success, and the creation of many large family fortunes. Through this new perspective, many individuals have come to understand, in a deeper way, what their parents' and grandparents' life experiences were all about.

DELINQUENCY

WORK WITH ADOLESCENT delinquents in the 1940s and 1950s provided some of the first real inroads into the uncharted terrain of family process. Therapists treated young people with compulsive delinquent behavior of a specific kind like stealing, fighting, or sexual promiscuity, by understanding how the activity met the needs of the mother or father without anyone being aware of it. Children identify not only with manifest behavior of their parents, but with the conscious and unconscious attitudes, wishes, and images that their parents feel, talk about, show, or perhaps actively deny in specific ways. As the child of either sex grows through the various stages, feelings and wishes a mother or father might have had in those same stages come up again in family conversations, and the parent sanctions and even invites the child to misbehave. The parent frequently does this by showing interest, and giving not merely undivided but rapt attention whenever the particular activities are talked about, even as the father or mother criticizes and "worries" about the child. A parent will question or warn too often, and the warnings will come at times when the *parent* is in distress. The parent and the child will feel guilty together about it, and all the other problems in the family will be temporarily forgotten.

With the adolescent, there is an unconscious or silent understanding between himself and his parent. With outsiders, one parent will frequently minimize the problem and be angry with the other for making "a big thing" of it. Inside the family, however, the parent expects and "knows" that the child is up to his old tricks. There is a warmth and a closeness in the preoccupation with details. Mother may want to know all about her daughter's sexual escapades, ending an hour-long conversation with a few disapproving remarks or, alternatively, she might explode and beat her daughter, who, underneath her anger, feels love in the contact from a mother who is otherwise cold. A father can reproach his son for running away, taking obvious pleasure in hearing the details of his exploits. There is an engagement between parent and child, closeness underneath the mutual guilt, blaming, and anger.

Youngsters who are drug addicts, as an example, frequently come from homes where one or both parents overindulge in one thing or another, like food, gambling, or alcohol. Yet the addict will always become the family scapegoat, bringing other family members closer, allowing them to deny and minimize their own problems. Recent research on teen-age delinquency by Dr. Melvin Singer shows that families with this pattern have very strict rules but very little policing and even less punishment for infractions. The children know the rules but do not take them seriously, learn to manipulate their way through life rather than anticipate reality and its consequences. They use their thought processes in a different way. Later on in life they may have great success in certain kinds of activities, yet sometimes, despite tremendous insight in knowing what other people are all about, they have problems in their relationships.

ADDICTION

DRUG AND ALCOHOL addiction is similar to other kinds of self-destructive overindulgences which give an inner "high" or balance to opposing feelings deep within the self. They include overeating, smoking, and gambling. People can be addicted to work and sometimes even to love. Anyone who has masturbated as an adolescent while feeling guilty about it, trying not to give in to the impulse, anyone who has dieted or tried to quit smoking, can understand what addiction is all about. There is a struggle between the conscious decision and an inner appetite, a struggle that, regardless of who wins at any one point in time, is quite likely to recur unless there is some change in the appetite, in what triggers it off, or in the person. It can be a response to a particular stressful situation, like being divorced. It can be an integral part of a life style, defining one's identity in a specific way by allowing a person to have an identity, to feel acceptance by one group and rejection by others. The kind of addiction, its chronicity and effect on a person's life can also be understood in terms of his life history and family. People who learn to handle or escape from feelings by overindulging choose an addiction according to what they observe in their families and what is available to them in their peer groups at school, at work or elsewhere. When under a strain that is difficult to cope with, we all use what we know and what is available. If the stress continues and the escape mechanism becomes self-reinforcing, like alcohol or drugs which require continued use to forestall withdrawal symptoms, or if there is a change in one's life style or self-image, the addiction replaces the additional stress as the problem.

In former years, psychiatrists theorized but seldom treated addicts and considered them difficult to work with. They were "orally fixated" and overindulged as infants with low frustration tolerance. They were not the usual kind of patient with good emotional equipment in a temporary neurotic conflict, but were, rather, deprived individuals, deprived of frustration early in life and not responsive to the usual type of individual treatment, which at times can be quite frustrating. Later it became obvious that people often can control their behavior when they understand something about it, why they like it and what it does for them. We sense that stress and availability of an outlet could make addicts of most of us and that real motivation for change and support while mastering addiction usually makes for success in controlling it. Doctors, for instance, who had the highest rate of drug addiction of any occupational group, had the highest cure rate because of the motivation for change and the support they received from their colleagues in the process.

While they are addicted, people relate to others around them in a specific way, giving out a number of messages, verbal or nonverbal. A cigarette in one hand, a drink in the other, with marijuana in his pocket, the individual controls his own gratifications and declares his independence from others. Yet his whole life style engages others—family, friends, and strangers—in a desperate way to help him meet his needs until they are exhausted or broke. He then avoids them and moves on to others, since it is the drug and not the people who are important, or so he tries to tell himself. He finds a peer group with needs similar to his own, and his life style becomes self-perpetuating.

Recently, through studying the families of drug addicts, it has been possible to look beneath the isolation, rebellion, and "pseudo-independence" of adults and young people with this kind of problem, and gain a deeper understanding of it. An addict's family frequently cuts itself off physically from the addict, yet mentally it is fully involved in his behavior. The structure of many addict families studied is the old familiar one in which the mother is overprotective, overindulgent, and enjoys a special relationship with the child. The father is usually weak, ineffectual, absent, or unreachable emotionally, with an addiction or preoccupation of his own, disappointing his wife and unavailable to his son while he was growing up. Despite what he says about his hatred of authority, the addict's search for controls in the form of incarceration, institutionalization, and militaristic drug programs can be seen as a search for a father.

Female addicts have similar family constellations, although an additional finding comes from a study in which the typical father tended to be inept, alcoholic, and sometimes sexually aggressive with his daughter, while the mother was usually competitive with the young woman as she was growing up.

Why is this family pattern so familiar and so characteristic of troubled families? It is similar to the system in some cases of schizophrenia and school phobia. Family researchers have looked for more specific aspects of structure and functioning for these conditions. Communication difficulties, for instance, have been associated with families of patients with schizophrenia, but beyond this finding, few other specifics are known. Perhaps this pattern, with overwhelming mothers and underinvolved fathers, is just a general kind of malfunctioning system, a family expression of a problem that individuals have in separating and achieving autonomy in their psychological functioning early in life.

A conflict involving feelings related to dependency is a common denominator for all these conditions. Perhaps, also, clear sexual identity is affected in one person, sense of reality in another, and appetite control in still another, because of the specific identity confusion of a parent, or the stage of development for a child at a time when some difficulty or change occurs in the family system. They all seem to be different aspects of the identification process that goes on very early in life, and all we can say now is that different kinds of interactions occur in a way too subtle to be understood.

The American version of drug abuse is noted for technical ingenuity, mass marketing, and perpetuation of a certain social stratification and value system. Since we value individuality and independence, the ability to control one's inner emotional state and take care of one's own gratifications is important for Americans. When drug use becomes an infringement upon others, however, it becomes threatening and infuriating because of the lack of control that is so obvious. Addicts for a time became scapegoats, "dope fiends," strange, unreachable creatures whose isolation, it was thought, should be punished by further isolation. Recently it has become possible for professionals and family members to realize that they get angry at addicts just as they get angry at anyone who is stubbornly self-destructive, out of control, resistant yet in need of help from others. We no longer insist on getting rid of addiction by getting rid of the addict, and we view behavior in its context, past, present, and future, to help these individuals discover possibilities for change in themselves. If the addict can accept himself, have some relationships, he can develop a sense of his own future. He and his family members will understand that he was not born with a permanent, insatiable hunger of one kind or another which will rule his life and make him distant from other people and unreachable.

What are the specifics, the context, what purposes are served by the alcoholic or the drug addict's behavior and identity? Addiction represents an attempt by the individual to deny separation, to be more whole, to recover or hold on to people the addict has lost or is about to lose. This is as true of the rebellious, "independent" adolescent drug addict as of the divorced or widowed middle-aged alcoholic male or female. Family structures that these individuals grew up in are of the "enmeshed" type, with closely knit members, each feeling a lot of responsibility and involvement in the behavior of others. Parents fail to set limits on their children or themselves; they deny problems and feelings; they merge with their children and seem not only to accept but to enjoy their children's overindulgence and lack of control. Later the addict feels that the outside world is a cold, uninviting place, and the drugs or alcohol provide the warmth and closeness that the old family provided.

As new people prove themselves undependable, as the addict begins to feel that nothing can fill his inner emptiness, that he cannot make it or get what he really wants in the world outside, he becomes more and more isolated, more and more involved with people from the past, with himself and with his own physical state of being. He gives up on people and turns to drugs because he can control them, have them whenever he wants, to give him pleasure. The addict hates himself for his dependency, and he hates others in his family for not being available more constantly. The frequent crises, the overdoses, the drunken driving, the arrests, are a way of testing the loyalty of the family members and of engaging them when no other way works. He reaches others in the family despite their sense of indignation at such inappropriate behavior, because on a deep level they are responsive and accept the behavior more than they think. It diverts everyone. It is consistent with the family's pattern and view of the world. Just as addiction can lead to poor relationships and personal losses, a loss as in divorce, bereavement, or physical illness (where there is a loss of health and independence) can lead to addiction. Families in which depression is chronic, where mourning is impossible and separation is not allowed, are characteristically "enmeshed," "glued together," cohesive families that have a high incidence of drug and alcohol use.

Family-oriented drug counselors look at adolescent drug abuse as a developmental crisis, a reaction to the failure of the individual to separate and go his own way at a time when *he* feels he should. As Dr. Jay Haley points out, when separation of adolescents is difficult for other family members, the problem can be solved for those others if something is wrong with the adolescent. If he proves himself "sick" in some way, the whole task and trauma and loss that parents feel in relation to their children when they grow up and leave is postponed or eliminated. The adolescent is functioning as if he were still a child, still at a time of his life when his parents' welfare meant everything to him and was more important than his own growth and well-being. Underneath his rebellion, the adolescent is happy to sacrifice himself when he sees that despite their disapproval, his depression-prone parents seem more comfortable when he is "the problem."

Therapists know that the crucial sessions with such a family are the ones where living arrangements, including separations and the conditions for an "open door" policy, are discussed. With the family approach now available in community-based clinics, with Alcoholics Anonymous, with methadone maintenance programs, and finally, with the heightened awareness of the dangers and broad context of drug abuse, addiction is less overwhelming and more manageable as a social problem than it was ten, or even five, years ago.

DEPRIVATION AMONG THE RICH

ACCORDING TO Drs. Roy Grinker Senior, Michael Stone, and Clarice Kestenbaum, certain young people from families in which there has been wealth for a number of generations experience depression, feelings of emptiness and abandonment, despair about the future, and problems trusting others in relationships, all symptoms typical of maternal deprivation early in life.

During their childhood years, these individuals were frequently isolated physically and socially from outside influences and opportunities. Their families were old-fashioned and tradition-bound, especially in their attitudes toward children. Like the poor in public homes and hospitals who grow up without parents, these wealthy children spend their early years in isolated estates, private institutions, or boarding schools, and feel abandoned by their parents, who are traveling or preoccupied, consumed not with making a living but with responsibility and social position. The physical needs of the children are met by professionals hired for the purpose. These children are short-changed as far as their emotional needs are concerned, and their early experience tends to shape their view of parenthood, so that when they have children, the pattern is repeated generation after generation. These affluent children are isolated not only from their parents but from outside agencies and society as a whole. They depend much more on siblings, often grow up in twosomes until school becomes a major interest in their lives.

Psychological development in this group of people is hindered. With little close emotional interaction with parents, children do not come to know and experience their feelings directly. There is structure in their lives but little expression of love or hate. Like some institutionalized children, they can learn to act rather than express their emotions. Some learn to focus on their bodies, not with pride and pleasure, but for reassurance and security against their feelings of emptiness. Family tragedies and financial reversals are times of warmth and togetherness for these children who yearn for parental contact. Sometimes the family structure, according to Stone and Kastenbaum, can also be characterized by great disparity in status and even in age between wife and husband, such that mother is like a sister and father like a grandparent.

As adults, these individuals can become hedonistic, unchallenged, and uncommitted to anyone or anything. Sometimes they marry, feel disappointment in the spouse, and turn to their children to protect them and fill their emotional needs or act out their own wishes.

Certain present-day trends, such as an overall increased standard of living, the disappearance of a professional servant class, the homogenization of our society, in which people of different socioeconomic groups go to similar schools, live in essentially similar "functional" households, travel as a nuclear-family unit when father or mother works as part of an organization, all may serve to eliminate this "institutionalization among the rich."

Only time will tell if day-care centers will have the dehumanizing effect on children of the middle class that professional child rearing has had on certain children of the affluent.

IMPRISONMENT

WHAT HAPPENS to children when their fathers go to prison? In a small but fascinating study, Dr. William H. Sack observed at first six and then a few dozen such families, and the results provide excellent insight into the specific pathways by which events affect people and how families cope with stress. It is never what happens to people that determines how it affects them but what resources they have inside and outside themselves to assist, support, and buffer them as they adapt to change. Some people can survive life in concentration camps while others become suicidal with trifling frustrations or even with success.

In families with imprisoned fathers that were studied, there was sometimes divorce soon after the incarceration; it was an opportunity for the wife to divorce her husband whom she blamed for an unsatisfactory or conflictual marriage. It is one of the many examples of how separation provokes other separations in families. The boys in the homes where there was divorce or marital turmoil got into trouble, often committing the very same crime that the father had committed, or they took on a certain characteristic trait of the father which they considered responsible for his imprisonment. Paternal separation became paternal deprivation and was structured permanently into the family. Like children of divorce, they took on qualities that they feared in the father who was now gone.

When the wife did not divorce and the family ship remained intact, the boys missed the father but did not imitate him. There was a painful absence of the father, but no paternal deprivation. Children acted up at school but only for a short time. (Two young brothers, for instance, seemed relieved and their own aggressive behavior ceased after a prolonged visit with their father during which they were able to ask and get answers to all the questions they had on their minds.) Feelings of anger and sadness about the father's absence were handled within the family, not outside of it. At first the children blamed the mother, and older children became bossy at home. If the mother did not become rejecting or inappropriate, the children soon stopped their blaming, began to feel better, and functioned well. The basic family structure, its capacity, endurance, and the long-standing emotional tone were more important than the separation itself in preventing difficulties for the children.

Finally, this group of families is significant for other reasons. Unlike other fatherless families where there is support from others in the community, these families have a powerful barrier between themselves and the outside. The reason for a father's absence is especially important to how the separation will affect others. If the mother and her children are ashamed, it becomes a harsh blow to their self-esteem to accept support from people in the extended family or community who they feel may be judging them. The imprisonment can be a painful secret, a cause of isolation of a family that is frequently on the move, that desperately needs support from community agencies and kin, but will not accept it. In fact, many of these families have moved frequently and usually move soon after the incarceration because of loss of income and the wish to be near the prison to visit more often. Even with this isolation, however, children in the families that remained intact with a father who continued as father even though absent were able to handle this crisis outside and inside themselves.

PSYCHOSOMATIC ILLNESSES

THE SHARP DISTINCTION that once existed between medical and emotional problems is no more. All of us know that illness makes us depressed, and depression and anxiety make us more susceptible to illnesses of various kinds. The distinction has disappeared for patients, for primary-care physicians, for researchers and planners. Occasionally, overworked interns or impatient technology-minded specialists may forget this fact. They might prefer fixing something in the here and now, wanting to see immediate results. They will forget the oneness of the mind and body and become annoyed with people or families who are chronically in distress in a poorly defined or ever-changing way. Yet when we examine statistics and when front-line health professionals think about their experience, it becomes obvious that 40 to 85 percent of visits to the doctor in his office, emergency room, or clinic are psychosomatic, stress-induced, or in some way related to an emotional conflict or a chronic psychosocial or domestic issue. Headaches, stomach aches, ulcers, colitis, high blood pressure, low blood pressure, heart disease, and allergies, all can have important emotional components. Overindulgence in alcohol, tobacco, or drugs, improper use of medication, poor eating habits, or living habits, and accident-proneness, all can create a vulnerability to repeated medical emergencies. Eating disturbances include overeating and its effects, as well as "anorexia nervosa," a condition of extreme weight loss in young women.

Stressful living habits can be more harmful than disturbed eating habits. For instance, a sense of time pressure and urgency combined with a stressful yet sedentary job may very well be more important in causing coronary-artery disease and heart attacks in young men than diet, smoking, or any other risk factor. Illnesses and accidents can occur in response to family events. Injuries which always seem to occur when a father is away on business can be the child's way of calling for his daddy, sometimes for himself, sometimes on behalf of someone else in the family.

Doctors refer patients for family therapy when they have one of the common psychosomatic illnesses, and medical or individual psychiatric treatment is not helping. A child with asthma takes his medication, but crisis after crisis continues to occur. An adolescent girl with diabetes goes into the hospital every few months in a diabetic coma. Father's alcohol abuse, Junior's drug abuse, Mother's overeating, or a young girl's "anorexia nervosa," all can be a malfunction of the normal nurturing activity of the family and should make professionals think of a family approach either with counseling, therapy or family organizations like Alcoholics Anonymous and its groups for family members such as Alanon or Alateen.

Therapy sessions with psychosomatically ill patients consist of understanding and restructuring the pattern that precipitates and maintains repeated medical crisis. What does such a crisis do for whom in the family? What is avoided that would otherwise be there? For instance, an eighty-pound adolescent girl starving herself to death in order to look "more attractive" concentrates on her diet and avoids dating relationships. Furthermore, with everyone in the house focused on food, the parents are not troubled by feelings about their daughter's growth, emerging femininity, and separation. The patient takes the weight of all the family's emotional interactions, and others are worried about her but relieved of other things.

Dr. Salvadore Minuchin and his colleagues have worked with families of patients with anorexia nervosa, diabetes, and asthma, and find that they are usually of the "enmeshed" type, with individuals overly involved with one another. Illness, especially in a child, is a way of being heard. The child sides with one parent or is the target of both, gets a position of attention or power, and when there is too much tension in the home, the emotional arousal is expressed by the child physiologically.

Even stress chemicals in the body called free fatty acids, which are high in parents when they argue, fall when the child enters the room, and rise in the child when the family shifts to talking about his illness.

Others in the family focus on the "sick" member to avoid real communication between themselves. Therapy consists of unhooking the child from this pathological position of power, allowing him to be a child once more, and working on the issues and communication that have been avoided. With this approach, family therapy as reported by Dr. Minuchin and his workers has been dramatically effective.

Dr. Lawrence Grolnick of the Family Studies Section of the Albert Einstein College of Medicine in the Bronx, New York, an expert on families with psychosomatic illness, has written insightfully that "there is a potent myth in these families. That the consequences of disagreement, of physical separation, or of any change may be fatal." He reminds us of how the English psychiatrist Dr. D. W. Winnicott "defined the key issue as the hyphen, i.e., the dissociation of a person's thoughts and feelings from his body and its needs," and he further points out how "splitting" someone's care between "one person arranging social changes, another managing hormone levels, the third treating the psychological conflicts" reinforces the "pathologic family system and the split within the person." Considering the kinds of things that make us ill in modern industrial communities—aging, and degenerative, stress-induced, and environmental diseases—such insights are crucial to our well-being as individuals and our future as a society.

I have found that one or another of these "special" problems exists to some degree in every family I have treated. All families must eventually deal with problems inherent in the life cycle: illness, decline, or death. Issues should be recognized, faced, and dealt with as they arise. People should be aware of the life cycle by keeping in ongoing contact with different generational levels in their own family. By following these guidelines as well as the principles outlined in the chapter on "Exercises in Understanding Your Family," people can deal with problems more easily, the family can move more smoothly from one phase to the next and can handle "special" problems when they arise.

IX

FAMILY THERAPY

FRANK RILEY, the head mortgage loan officer at East Chicago Savings, hung up the phone and sat back in his chair. He wondered about the DeMarcos. What was going on? Nancy did not sound like herself. She sounded crazy. Her family was four months behind in mortgage payments, and foreclosure proceedings had begun. Yet she had just told him on behalf of her father, who was "not available" that she had half the money for a mortgage payment but had spent the other half on some new dresses. Nancy was fifteen, a school friend of his daughter's, and everyone in his family liked her. As he hung up the phone he thought she had sobbed. He looked over some loan applications for a few minutes but couldn't concentrate. He called Nancy back. She picked up the phone on the first ring.

"What's the matter?" he asked. "What's going on, Nancy?"

"Things aren't so good at home," Nancy said. "My grandfather is always out . . . and I . . ." She broke down. "I just can't take care of her anymore . . . my grandmother . . . it's too much."

Frank was in tears himself, yet he felt better now that something was out in the open. "Nancy, can I make a suggestion? Can I call Father Douglas?"

Nancy said okay. She lived with her maternal grandparents Al and Rose De Marco and her two uncles, Al Junior and Vince. Her mother had been a beautiful woman, an actress and a model with a promising career. After her divorce she began drinking heavily, and one night three years earlier, while on vacation in Florida, she went swimming alone and drowned. It took a week to find her body.

A year earlier Nancy's grandmother Rose had gone into Chicago shopping and disappeared. Rose had high blood pressure. She either had a stroke and fell in the street, or was hit by a car. She was taken to a hospital without identification, had amnesia, went, after a few weeks, to a large psychiatric hospital upstate for six months, and finally was taken to a nursing home.

Her husband, Al Senior, and the entire family had searched everywhere. He even went back to Italy; he suspected family members of hiding her. He checked records in hospitals, police stations, and newspapers. Meanwhile, Rose's powers of mind came back little by little. Fragments of memories came until she remembered her maiden name, her address as a child, and finally even her married name. After eleven months Al received word from the nursing home where Rose had been taken that she might be there. He drove there at once and took her home that day.

Rose was paralyzed on one side, had trouble speaking but seemed to recognize everyone and seemed happy to be home. The family was ecstatic. Everyone decided that it would be Nancy's job to take care of her grandmother.

The mood at home changed after Rose had been in the house for just a few weeks. Al began drinking heavily and missed work day after day. Vince stopped going to school, talked about joining the service but spent most of the time hanging around the street corner waiting for Friday nights and the weekends. He looked as if he was on drugs.

After a month at home Rose had another stroke and her condition worsened. Al Senior and Vince stayed out of the house as much as possible now. Al Junior was back and forth between home and his girlfriend's apartment. Rose missed appointments with her doctor and rehabilitation therapist, and Nancy had no way of getting her there.

Father Douglas went and visited the family. He talked to them all.

The household was quiet and depressing. Al apologized that he and his family had not been to church in a while. He felt very guilty about it—too guilty, in fact. Father Douglas had known plenty of Italian men who didn't go to mass, some of them right in his own family. He wondered what else Al and his sons might be feeling guilty about.

He listened as they spoke. Rose complained that nobody helped her and as she talked everyone seemed to be in great pain. Nancy complained that she had to take care of her grandmother and manage the house at the same time, all by herself. Nancy seemed depressed, while Al and his sons were fidgety. They talked little. They seemed annoyed that they had to be there. They had "more important things to do." Yet each and every one asked Father Douglas to come back.

On his second visit Father Douglas felt a strong urge to cheer them up, to make suggestions and mobilize them. He thought hard about what troubled these people. Rose had been a matriarch, the backbone of the family. They had fought, struggled, and paid dearly to find her. Yet now that she was back they were falling apart. Rose needed medical treatment and Nancy needed help. Father Douglas arranged for homemaking and visiting-nurse services; also an ambulette to take Rose to the hospital. The family accepted this help, but they were still not mobilized.

On the third visit Father Douglas almost had to drag Vince and young Al out of bed. It was as if they were doing him a favor by talking with him. They and their father said very little, watched, and waited. They seemed to want him there, they wanted his help, but they were not going to make it easy for him. They would make him feel the way they felt. They seemed to be holding on for dear life, walking a tightrope. With Father Douglas there they could be around Rose more easily. They hated being around her. *That* was what they felt guilty about.

On his fourth visit Father Douglas realized he was frustrated, almost annoyed. He had an urge to punish these men and criticize them. After a few minutes he asked about Al Senior's parents, and how it was when they died. He asked about Nancy's mother, who had always said she wanted to be a "pretty corpse." He heard about her shame, her divorce, and her disappearance. Suddenly he felt the "click," the "moment of truth" that family therapists feel when they know *emotionally* what a family problem is all about: this family depended on Rose and could not deal with her decline. She was supposed to take care of everyone else. When she was lost, her disappearance had been a challenge to the men. But now, here at home, the family had to deal with the gradual loss of hope for her recovery, and they just could not accept it. Father Douglas realized they needed support, not criticism; care, not direction. He sat back in silence for a moment and told them, quite suddenly, that he thought they had all done a great job and that nothing more was to be done. They had brought her home. She was where she belonged. It was up to God now. The men were shocked, silent. Al Senior began to cry quietly and Nancy went over to comfort him. After a few minutes he stopped and talked about Rose, the way she had been. By the time the visit ended, they all said that they felt relieved. Father Douglas suggested that they might bring Rose to rehabilitation at the hospital to get some relief because they should not try to handle this whole thing themselves. Nancy decided she would go to a group for young people while Rose was in rehabilitation therapy. Father Douglas also wanted to call Al Senior's older sister in Detroit to tell her about the whole situation. He knew this sister from childhood and knew that she would want to hear about it. He would find someone for Al the way Al had found Rose for the family.

The next day Vince was arrested for smoking marijuana in public. Everyone mobilized around the new crisis; they got him a lawyer and they learned the charge would be dropped when he agreed to go to drug classes. By the following week Al Senior had stopped drinking ("I have no taste for it"), had been back at work for most of the week, and called home regularly ("I have to stay on top of Vince's situation"). Vince was back in school. He had no choice. Even his friends knew about his drug charge. Two mortgage payments had been made with the help of the family in Detroit, and Nancy was no longer depressed. She still took care of her grandmother. In fact, she and everyone else in the family spent more time with Rose, not requiring or expecting anything from her in return and not feeling guilty about not being able to cure her. Nothing in the family had changed; they just looked at everything in a new way. They were not failures. There was nothing to feel guilty about, no need to drown the guilt in wine or pot, and no need to punish themselves by losing their home.

IN THE DAY BEFORE the psychotherapy revolution—before the defamation of the family and the erosion of our value system became routine—families helped each member cope with expected crises associated with growth and change, and unexpected difficulties as well. Each person's problems triggered responses in others that led to a new emotional equilibrium. For instance, an adolescent experiencing sexual urges rejects his parents in order to keep distant from them; it is practice for the step of separation that comes after adolescence. Mother and Father, feeling rejected, would turn toward each other more—with love or blame or both— but in any case, they were closer. All the challenges that people experience in their lives, from the growth cycle and from the world outside, were mediated through the family.

The effort to understand and deal with emotional distress in a family context is centuries old and present in every culture. Confucius emphasized the importance of the family, and so did the Greek myths. Ancient Hawaiian families met to discuss the problems of an individual. In our own culture, family relationships and obligations were worked and reworked throughout the Old Testament and the New: Adam and Eve, Cain and Abel, Ruth and Naomi. The Bible dealt with almost every conceivable family issue and gave an ethical dimension to negotiations between family members and the social contracts between families themselves.

With the birth of modern medicine in the nineteenth century, researchers focused on infections and deficiency diseases. They began to understand human physiology and pathology in a comprehensive way, and to effectively treat and prevent diseases with techniques previously unimaginable. The emphasis was on anatomy and physiology, and the scientific framework was specific cause and effect or "linear causality."

It was in this climate of anatomy and physiology that Sigmund Freud diagnosed and treated patients previously unaffected by this scientific revolution, and he developed the first practical depth psychology. His observations, as well as theoretical and clinical work over the course of fifty years, led to the founding and development of psychoanalysis, which became the foundation of modern psychiatry. It became *the* framework for research, understanding, treatment, and prevention of emotional disturbances in people.

In his early clinical efforts Freud focused on patients with one kind of nervous disorder—hysteria and hysterical paralysis. In spite of the fact that he worked in a setting where the medical model was the only relevant and authoritative one, his key concepts included the existence and importance of the feelings and fantasies that people themselves were not aware of—the unconscious; the existence of sexual interest and activity in young children; the multiple causes of any thought, feeling, and activity in the mind; and the importance of dreams. He expanded the relevance of his work to other illnesses and research, and most important, to a way of understanding mental phenomena that preceded illnesses and were in fact a part of normal development.

Although Freud wrote to some extent about society and civilization, he said, curiously, very little specifically about the family. Sometimes he noticed that patients got better when they were removed from their families. The family influenced and even seemed to *need* the illness in the patient. Later, in *Totem and Taboo,* he focused on marriage and the relationships with in-laws. He noted how feelings in one person could be worked out in a relationship between two others in the family, and this thinking foreshadowed important ideas later in the century about how children act on behalf of their parents' unconscious wishes.

More important than direct references, however, Freud's work emphasized early childhood experiences and family relationships. His idea of making sense out of apparently incomprehensible symptoms is perhaps the most basic and widespread principle of family therapy today. Even Freud's treatment of little Hans through sessions with the child's father can be viewed as perhaps as one of the first modern family therapy treatment cases.

Freud's detachment from the family of the patient is a result of
two things. First, psychoanalysis as a treatment technique emphasized "transference," the intense relationship that blossomed
between the patient and the analyst in which the analyst is less a
real person and more a composite of the patient's past important
figures. The analyst encourages this process by remaining neutral
and impassive. Freud found that transference and its exploration
was the most powerful curative force.

Second, the intellectual environment and the value system of
the times, with its emphasis on individualism, the medical model,
and linear cause and effect rather than thinking in terms of circular feedback systems kept analysts from involving themselves in
their patients' lives and families. Nevertheless, Freud's work laid
the foundation for modern psychiatric techniques and were in-
strumental in the dramatic expansion in the social sciences which
gave rise to modern family therapy.

The contribution of Freudian theory is nothing less than the
elucidation of the mechanisms by which people relate to other
people. Although the transference relationship is most clearly
seen in psychoanalysis, aspects of transference are a part of relationships with other people in everyone's life. The infinite variety
and the specificity of emotional responsiveness due to transference, the feelings, attitudes, and expectations of others that are
the result of our own past relationships, allow us to recognize the
impact of the past on the present. We can understand, for instance, why we instantly like or dislike, or trust, or trust without
liking, or like without trusting, people of a particular type or sex;
also why we fall in love or out of love (which can happen when a
person fails to live up to transferential expectations). Without
such knowledge there can be no understanding of institutions like
marriage, groups, or even society in general.

In addition to transference, psychoanalytic theory gave us an
understanding of "projections," i.e., one's own feelings are "pro-
jected" on, or put on, another, usually an intimate, because the
feelings are for some reason unacceptable to oneself. A man can
consider his wife dependent, for instance (usually encouraging
her to be so), as a way of handling his own dependency feelings,
which he would rather disavow. A woman can blame her husband

for devaluing her because of her femininity, while it can be she herself who is troubled by feelings of inferiority as a woman. When we relate to intimates as projections of ourselves (and we all do it to one degree or another), we usually *hate* them but also *need* them a great deal. (As the song goes: "You always hurt the one you love, the one you shouldn't hurt at all . . .") There is also not much the other person can do about anger, arguments, or dissatisfaction. Changes often frighten everyone in the family and are resisted by all.

In addition to transference and projection, there is a whole repertoire of mechanisms by which people handle the feelings they have for others. Freud gave us the anatomy, the physiology, and the very language for emotionality in relationship which became the theoretical foundation for later research in child development, social sciences, clinical psychological medicine, and the human-growth movement.

In the 1940s, psychoanalysts noticed that when a patient began changing there were intense reactions in other family members. If the "patient" got better, it was as though a separation had taken place, even if he stayed in the family. Someone else often emerged as the "problem." Sometimes a person would go to a psychoanalyst, fall in love with him or her, and get divorced. Or a patient would fall in love with the analyst, begin to hate him, after which the patient's violent marriage would quiet down. At least one analyst, Bela Mittelmann, began seeing married couples in simultaneous individual analyses to understand and control the effects of the individual's change on these marriages.

During this period, developments in other research areas influenced mental-health care. General Systems Theory was a young science at the time, but it supplied a framework for a giant leap forward in the technological sciences.

This theory was a way of conceptualizing the world. It taught that all things, whether concrete or abstract—the red blood cell, the heating system of a home, or the mental health of a certain county—could be understood as a collection of parts which existed in a certain relationship to one another. In some way the parts communicated any changes in their status to one another by positive or negative feedback so that a change in one part affected other parts of the system. Systems tended to stay in a certain kind of balance, a "homeostasis," sometimes resisting change, sometimes incorporating it. There was also a hierarchy in which parts of the system could be broken down into systems themselves. For instance, the individual is part of the family, the cardiovascular system is part of the individual, the heart is part of the cardiovascular system, and the ventricle is part of the heart.

In relation to mental-health care, the first application of this new theory was to group therapy. Leaders could understand how and why members of a group related to one another, and how groups seemed to take on a life of their own, somehow becoming "greater" or "different from the sum of their parts."

In the 1950s, people doing different things in different places, unaware of one another's activities, suddenly learned that work with families was going on all over the country. Child-guidance counselors, psychiatrists involved in the treatment of schizophrenia, delinquency, and problems of adolescence, and crisis therapists, all shared experiences and ideas concerning family structure and operations, and the nature of change. They found the family approach often more effective, more quickly and less traumatically, than any other approach used with problem patients. First of all, not only were families intimately involved in the problem of a particular member, sometimes they caused or encouraged it without anyone realizing it. Second, family members were concerned and available for help on a twenty-four-hour-a-day basis; they simply needed guidance and support. There were always some problems—guilt and the ever-present blaming phenomenon. But these could usually be overcome.

In 1970 the Group for the Advancement of Psychiatry published the results of a poll of family therapists active in this country to learn who they were, who influenced them, and how they worked. Family therapists could be placed on a continuum between those concerned with individual emotional factors and those who viewed the family only as a system with a structure of its own that needed reshaping. Family therapy clearly was not just another psychiatric treatment method but was different in a most basic way, focusing not on patients themselves but on the social context and the system, with a secondary goal of prevention of emotional and medical difficulties.

Therapists of the different schools were quite vocal in their opinions of one another. Psychoanalytically trained psychiatrists considered the "systems" people silly, superficial, and esoteric, resistant to feelings inside patients and in themselves. Systems therapists invariably replied, "They just don't understand systems. Psychoanalysis is old-hat, anyway, with its fancy language; 'resistance' and 'transference' and 'insight.' " (Systems people use simple language like "pseudo-mutuality" and "equi-finality" and multidirectional partiality.") Therapists declare themselves with their language and quickly recognize friend or foe according to ideology.

In their practice they were quite flexible. Some therapists brought in anyone who was important to the treatment situation, not just the nuclear family. They frequently made home visits, and psychiatrists would prescribe drugs, sometimes for family members other than the individual patient. Co-therapy at that time was common and was used by 80 percent of the therapists at one time or another. The purpose of it was to provide models, since co-therapists were usually male and female. It was also important to keep track of the material, more voluminous than in individual sessions. Finally, co-therapy helped the therapists keep their own emotional balance and objectivity. Clearly, family therapy was not just a treatment method but a new premise about cause, cure, and the human condition.

Therapists use any techniques which might be helpful. We use microanalysis and video-tape sessions with families for many reasons. Sometimes we use it to show people things about themselves that they would not believe unless they saw them. Sometimes we need video tape for research on family communications, verbal and nonverbal. At other times we need video tape to understand in the deepest way possible what is going on at a particular moment in a family's life.

Virginia had come to the doctor because she trusted him. She wanted to talk about her Aunt Mary, who was drinking heavily and would not go out of the house. Her two aunts, Mary and LuAnn, lived in town, while Virginia and her three children lived on a small farm nearby. A week later Doris, Virginia's fifteen-year-old daughter, came to the doctor and said her mother was depressed. Three days after that, Virginia returned and said that

Doris had been depressed ever since her father's death one year earlier. The doctor was a family practitioner, and both he and the social worker he worked with had training as family therapists. He recommended that Virginia come in with her whole family.

In the session Mary complained about her arthritis, LuAnn about her heart trouble. Virginia complained about Doris and her teenage misbehavior. No one talked about *her* own feelings or depression, only what they suspected in each other. Virginia complained that Doris stayed out late and went to a discotheque with her boyfriend. Also, she might have been smoking marijuana. These complaints all lasted about twenty minutes. In a quiet moment the doctor asked Virginia about her childhood, how it was for her when she was Doris' age. She had been raised by Theresa, her grandmother, the matriarch of the family, who had died two years earlier. Last week was the anniversary of her death. Suddenly twelve-year-old Susan burst into tears. This was the moment that was frozen on the video-tape machine later on, the key moment of the session. Virginia broke down too and went on to describe her grief at her grandmother's death, her mixed feelings toward her mother, her yearning for her dead father, her own drinking as well as her father's. Mary and LuAnn joined in the grief for Theresa, the work that had been delayed and avoided for two years. The problem was originally felt as Doris' "rebellion," but it wasn't rebellion, it was a conflict over Doris' growth, which was felt as another loss. It also combined with the anniversary reaction.

Why had Susie burst out at that moment? She was young and these feelings were allowed at her age, in this family. What made her sad? She was sad over the loss of a great-grandmother she loved. But she knew her only vaguely. She was depressed over her sister Doris' disappearance into adulthood. She was sad, most of all, however, over the change in her mother and the loss of her mother that came with thoughts of Theresa. She grieved for her mother, to prevent her mother from grieving; she grieved to regain her mother. This was what happened in that instant. In the safety of the doctor's office Susie's efforts at avoidance of pain failed, and for half an hour or so, her mother felt feelings in a direct way that were making everyone in the family upset. After the session Susie, Doris, and their brother, Roger, had their mother's love in a way in which they had not had it in two years.

HOW THERAPISTS WORK

IN A GENERAL WAY the approach varies according to the orientation of the therapist and the need of the family at the moment. Some take a full "longitudinal" history of the people and of the family, including the two families that preceded it or were blended into or cut off from it. These workers attempt to put any specific problem in perspective. They look in the family history for patterns, repeated traumas, or reactions to normal events in the life cycle, such as things that might happen in a family when the sons turn eighteen or the daughters turn fourteen.

Those who focus on past history sometimes emphasize the fact that a parent of an individual in the room can be an old internalized parental figure as well as a new parent existing in the present day, that old internalizations are easier to rework, often with the parent present in the here and now.

Other therapists take a "cross-sectional" view or "living snapshot," starting with the problem at hand, going from there to the context of the problem, the repercussions in the family, and finally to an understanding of how the problem fits into the equilibrium. They try to learn how having the "problem" really solves other unacknowledged problems that could emerge in other individuals in the family. For instance, of all the situations that therapists deal with, perhaps the most common is the one in which people create problems for themselves or others in order to avoid separation. People who do not "make it" for one reason or another often end up staying close to home, dependent on parents, or they lead constricted lives in a kind of self-imposed exile maintaining a fixed image of others in the family.

Feelings can be contagious as well as reactive. Children might get depressed because a parent is depressed or they might "act up" because a parent is depressed. These therapists want to know all about the problem; why the family seeks to do something about it *now*.

A third approach, used by certain well-known therapists with vast experience working with families and a well-thought-out conceptual framework, is to jump right into the stuff of therapy, negotiating and attempting change. If they think the family can handle the strain, their framework quickly becomes an agenda for the family. These "experts" present a dazzling array of family therapeutic styles prominently displayed in teaching programs and audio-visual materials. They constitute a veritable "super-market" of family therapy techniques. Some construct family "genograms"—diagrams of the family and its two different families of origin, and each of *their* two families of origin—exploring what the patterns are that are being "recycled," who represents whom (for instance, who is named after whom; which child seems to be "just like" his father or mother or grandmother). The his- torically oriented go back three or more generations into the past and guide the family members in their social and emotional archaeology. They want to know what relationships are being repeated down the generational tree.

Others focus on communication patterns between members, learning what feelings are obstructed either inside the self or within the family framework. They look upon improved feeling tone and empathy as the most desirable goal. Still others help the family accomplish certain tasks, such as working on an unresolved grief or mourning reaction.

Some talk about inner and outer "space" in the family. Others talk of the bonds or obligations or legacies between family members past and present. Some family therapists control the meet-ings. They are the doctors and the *family* is the patient. Others join in, are enveloped by the family, usually to a point, and then step back to show the family what it does to individuals like him-self and presumably like themselves. Still, despite differences in terminology and theoretical construct, the approach to any prob-lem is through the family, the *natural* interpersonal context; and the goals affect everyone in the family.

A detailed structure-function approach to analyzing the family will be presented shortly. At this point, one can say that in think-ing about a family, a therapist wants to know what the individuals are like and how the family functions as a system. How well does it meet the needs that all human beings have and that those in this family in particular have?

First of all, who are the individuals in this family? Where are they and where is the family in its developmental cycle or life course, and where should they be or might they be, given the time, place, and people involved? How do the individuals relate to one another? Do they view one another as separate, autonomous, and flexible, or do they deal with distortions, images of their own making, feeling the others as hopelessly rigid, incapable of change?

As a system, how does the family accomplish its tasks? What is the power structure? Who is boss? How does the boss get his or her way, and how flexibly is power shared? Healthy families are neither dictatorships nor democracies. How effectively do family members communicate? How comfortable is everyone with all the feelings that human beings have? Do expressions of anger or sexual or dependency feelings upset others? What is the mood of the family? These in general are the questions that therapists try to answer when they think about family functioning.

The family approach to solving the problems of psychiatric and medically vulnerable patients is the mainstay of many service agencies throughout the country. As therapists refined their techniques and understood more about normal family development and normal "crisis," they became better able to help families distinguish "growing pains" from pathology and resolve "normal" crises. They play a major role in the prevention of social, psychological, and physical illnesses.

This expansion of family awareness was the result of the family revolution of the 1950s, a movement which has survived the intense social ferment and anti-family feeling of the 1960s, and stimulated much of the "human-growth experience": marriage encounters, Parent-Effectiveness-Training, and sex therapy. Family Therapy clearly is not just another psychiatric treatment method but is different in a most basic way, opening up our view of the human condition, focusing not only on "patients" themselves, but on the social, historical, and ethical field as well.

X

HOW YOU CAN ANALYZE YOUR FAMILY

Now THAT YOU'VE COME this far in examining family processes, you may be curious about your own family. Do not rush to categorize yourself or your family. All families change over time and vary even with your own mood or vantage point at the moment. Instead, use the following parameters in order to make a careful and informed evaluation.

In evaluating a family, the first thing one does is define the boundary between the family and the outside. Who's in and who's out, and how is that determination made? Is the boundary impermeable, with family members who are unable to trust anyone outside? (Even Don Corleone, in *The Godfather*, had an adopted son, whom he trusted as much as his natural sons. He called anyone whom he trusted "family," and considered all others outsiders.) Or is there no boundary at all, with a chaotic family structure and instant intimacy with family members who love and even live with anyone anytime?

Where and how do family members live? What is their home like? Who sleeps where? How much time does each one spend alone (with what degree of comfort), and how much time with outsiders? One tries to get a sense of the inner and outer space of the family and its members.

Focus on the individuals (the parts) as well as the family system (the whole) by defining the members of the family the way a "demographer" would. Who is in the family? Who am I and who are we, as others might see us and define us? What would census takers or demographers think about us in relation to number, sex, age, religion, class, and place of residence? What do we say about our categories, what do we know that we don't say, and what would we like to say? For instance, a person might think of herself as a "middle-aged upper-middle-class American housewife who married down." A man might say, "I married down but my wife is more American." I have even heard, "We both married down." There is an infinite variety in the combinations one might hear in reference to these categories; and your family's self-concept has important implications concerning the degree of integration into the community. It relates to values, levels of comfort, "problems" of members, and overall resourcefulness.

If you listen to people put themselves into "family" categories you might hear: "Mother was a Lodge." "I'm black and I'm proud," from a five-year-old whose grandfather says, "He's black and he's proud; I'm just a country nigger but I put his father through Amherst." "My family is German-Jewish, my wife's is Polish." "We're Italian-American." "Calabrese." "Barese." "Hardhats." "Jewish intellectuals." "Stone New Yorkers." "Everyone knows who we are."

These characteristics also relate to other family operations, such as rules of communication. Old adages and myths can sometimes refer to earlier realities. ("Children should be seen and not heard," and "The Cabots speak only to the Lodges, and the Lodges speak only to God.")

You have to know where you come from to know where you are going, what values you have as a family, and how appropriate or "congruent" they are with those in the families around you.

Conflicts in your family may vary according to categories, values, and "congruence." For instance, upper- and lower-class families seem to tolerate divergence or idiosyncrasy in members better than middle-class families, where the boundary between the family and the outside is more rigid.

Families are based on marriages, and marriages are based on a social and genetic selection process that determines family style, success, and type of dysfunction. Family style can determine class parameters as much as class affects the family. In their classic work in the 1950s, Drs. Redlich and Hollingshead proved how patients with certain mental illnesses such as schizophrenia tended to drift to a lower socioeconomic status, and how mental-health professionals tended to limit their personal involvement with such patients by using drugs and hospitalization rather than psychotherapy. In a sense, they might have been in collusion with this drift.

More recently some researchers have alluded to the high productivity and wealth of people with manic-depressive disease, especially of the controlled manic type.

Finally, there are important connections between demography and other features of family analysis accounting for mixed class characteristics; for instance, those who *must* marry outside their religion or race or social class because of unresolved feelings and primary attachment to the original family.

One defines the family in this way in relation to current family, family of origin, and their families of origin. Such an analysis takes on richness when there are three or more generations involved, and certain patterns emerge almost immediately.

It is best to use the large-scale, multi-generational time dimension rather than the one-generational "life cycle" view described earlier. Finally, those who are without family roots that are easily traceable should know that in my experience, despite wars, holocausts, natural disasters, and emigrations, family histories are often more easily obtainable than individuals ever imagined.

Adopted children, especially if they were adopted in infancy, share, except for genetic influences, in the family environment, how *they* structure *it* and how *it* affects *them*, exactly as natural children. Family members are "in each other's bones" in the same way. There are additional features, however, which relate not so much to the biological parents of the adopted as they do to the feelings about the circumstances of adoption; for instance, infertility of one parent, the mother's experience with pregnancy or absence of it. The infant, however, exists in fantasy and is born the day he arrives in the family the same way a biological child does.

One next considers the individuals in the family. How does each one feel and relate to others, and how does each experience the family? What does each one say about how they seem to outsiders? What are the family themes, overt and covert? Overt themes are what they talk about: money, activities, who gets what, who is the best, who is being unfair, who made a mistake. Covert themes are emotionally charged. "Will we starve?" "Can we trust one another?" "Can we touch each other, will we destroy each other?" "Would we really care if one of us left?" "Could we go on if one of us died?"

On an individual basis, what are the significant things about each individual in the family, his personality, his early experiences, especially as they relate to emotional development and early relationships?

What were his mother and father like? What about his sibling relationships? What were they like and where did he fit in? Where did he get his ideas about what men and women are like? And what did he observe between his father and his mother?

Particular individuals might have been designated by their name, birth order, or physical appearance to play a certain role in the family, and I shall elaborate on this when I discuss roles.

I have already discussed the life cycle of the individual. Suffice it to say here that one looks for obvious traumas, repetitive patterns, vulnerability of certain members or subgroups, such as a particular sex or age group, for instance, boys or adolescents or anyone at the time he reaches his thirteenth or eighteenth birthday. Each step in an individual's life cycle can be thought of as a crisis, as Erickson wrote: "Simultaneously a time of danger and a time of positive growth."

Therapists in most family clinics throughout the country can attest to the fact that every family has a vulnerability to a particular kind of stress related to the stage and life cycle of certain members. Most family therapy in this country today is short-term, helping families to resolve these crises.

Finally, you can attempt to determine the "hidden agendas" in your family; that is, the thought, feeling or fantasy, usually a fear or wish that is most constantly there but not spoken about. It is a kind of sum total of the covert themes in the family, and can range from pervasive fears such as "Are we likable?" "Don't criticize us," "Whatever you do, don't raise your voice," to myths like "Father's not weak, Mother's not depressed, we're all happy, aren't we?" or "We are powerful," "We're all special, and none of us is mediocre," or "See how we never lose control." A very common one is: "We always do whatever Mother [Father] wants, and we do it of our own free will, because among other perfections, Mother [Father] is not controlling."

What are the value conflicts between different subgroups in a family, and how typical are they? There are always some—for instance, between older and younger generations, between the sexes —and in a sense the conflicts define the subgroups which are part of all functioning families. Are there value conflicts within the individual—for example, in a woman who wants to be a mother fully available to her children, yet wishes for autonomy and success as a working woman? Tolerance for conflicts and flexibility in handling them are more important than the particular conflicts themselves.

Next, one looks at the family as a system, with its subgroupings, the parental system, the sibling system, the males, the females, the strong, the weak, the individual subsystems, the people in their roles, like husband (leader or follower, lover, provider), father (disciplinarian, nurturer, companion), wife (leader or follower, lover, nurturer), mother (nurturer, disciplinarian, companion). Each child in age- and sex-appropriate roles. Internal structures of the family system are defined by communication based on these role relationships, and include boundaries (between sexes, for instance, when father and son do things the "gals" don't do, while mother and daughter can know things the men "just wouldn't understand"; also, there are boundaries between generations: "What's the matter with these kids today?" or "Mom and Dad just wouldn't understand.") Subunits of the family include coalitions (partnerships), pairings (loving couples), and splits (persistent hostilities). Triangles are also a common formation and relate particularly to problems about jealousy and competition.

For a number of years, communication has been the focus of attention for many researchers, not only in family therapy but in all the psychological sciences. Those who study communications in minute detail, the "how" and the "why," as well as the "what" of communication, tell us that inside the family most messages are not "new information" conveyed from one family member to another. Communication seems to have a different function and can be viewed as a form of behavior, a transaction between different family members, just as behavior, thought, feelings, and even symptoms can be viewed as communication. It is important because it is the "how" of important behavior and is defined by (and itself defines through feedback mechanisms) the relationships between the members of the family. Thus, messages have "report" and "command" functions.

"It's cold" is a report and can also be an instruction to take an overcoat. The command function defines relationships and establishes rules whereby relationships can be understood, especially concerning two of the most important parameters of family function: power and caring.

Intimately related to the development of self-image and of the thinking process in the infant, communication styles reflect the thought patterns, goals, and general social adjustment of family members and define the boundary of the family as a whole. Finally, the greatest importance of communication lies not in what the expert can learn about the family from its observation, but in what family members can do with a few basic principles, sometimes with professional help, sometimes without it, to improve the emotional climate and functioning of the family. Unlike unconscious processes, communications are accessible, although most of the time we are unaware of what or why we are communicating. A communication may relate to an unconscious feeling or attitude, but what we communicate is right out in front of us, if only we can learn to hear and understand ourselves and others. In other words, communication reflects what is going on inside us that is unknown and perhaps frighteningly powerful. It can be a new "royal road" to our inner psychological processes and liberate us from our unknown selves.

There is a growing body of literature on improving communication in families, and some therapists, like Virginia Satir, are masterful in understanding, translating, and expediting new communications and emotional possibilities from within individuals and between family members. Even without understanding deep layers of causation or hurt, family members can function much more effectively by following the principles of good communication (see Chapter 3).

In evaluating messages, one thinks about how much is new information being processed and how much is usual, a redefinition of aspects of the family system. Adaptive families seem to process a greater proportion of new information, while maladaptive families seem to use communication to constantly rework and redefine relationships in the family system. The paradigm for all such communication in malfunctioning families is "I told you so," a remark which among other things is useless in itself, yet punishes the family member who hears it, brings him closer, and warns him to stay close for fear of the future. It is a reflection of the fearfulness and sense of inadequacy of the person saying it.

There are four channels of communication: verbal, paraverbal ("between the lines"), nonverbal (body language), and action (hitting, doing, etc.). Second, clarity and focus are also important. Are the messages clear or tangential (change into something else) or even amorphous (change into nothing) or just confusing? How do they change over time? Are messages congruent with others on the same topic? Are they logical and understandable? Is it clear that everyone takes responsibility for his own message?

Who sends and who receives what kind of information and with what effect? What does the communication pattern tell about the pair involved? Are they symmetrical (are they similar) or complementary (matching one's weaknesses with the other's strengths)?

I outlined some rules of healthy communication in Chapter 3, "Exercises in Understanding Your Family." I have also discussed other systems' aspects of the family, like power structure, emotional tone, and seeing others and our families as others see us.

Just as one obtains a history of the personality development of certain individuals, one also tries to work out a developmental history of the family and its phases. How did the spouses first meet? What did they see in each other? What did they imagine?

What were courtship, marriage, and pregnancy like? Were there any deaths in the family? Are their parents' or children's families just as important as their own, blended though they are with another family of origin?

How does the family system change to meet any new development, from usual crises like illnesses or deaths of family members or the separations that are part of the life course, to the unusual crises like wars, natural disasters, or economic disruptions? For instance, did social changes disturb the function of the family as a whole? Events like wars, Depressions and migrations are society's crisis points as marriages and births are individual ones. Did such events cause separations, especially from children, or affect the emotional climate or sense of security of any member? How old were the children and what must have been the experience of each one? Wars do not cease affecting us when they are over. The repercussions in terms of disruption, separation, depression, and threat determine the emotional tone and tasks of families for generations. The societal healing process after a war can take decades. It can even go wrong and lead us from one war to another, as World War I led to World War II. It can affect a society's value system, its ideology, its mythology in a permanent and decisive way. Individuals can feel the effects of a war twenty years after its end, in a parent's chronic low-grade depression or in a family structure where a child and mother have a closeness that excludes the father, sometimes creating problems for the adolescent when it is time for him to leave home.

According to Dr. Samai Davidson, children who have never seen a concentration camp, born years after the end of World War II to parents who survived the Holocaust, can have depression, anxiety, and even nightmares of Nazi persecution and life in the camps. They have "concentration camp survivor's syndrome." The mechanism probably involves parents who lost relatives, friends, home and country, were emotionally devastated, numb, unable to grieve, who became overprotective and overinvolved in the lives of their children.

Emigration, a family's change from one world to another, also affects people for generations. America is a society of immigrants, with a hierarchy based on how long one's family has been in the country and where it emigrated from. Americans who trace their roots in an effort to know themselves better feel their work is incomplete until they find the ancestor who came to this country, the circumstances, and the experience of this original voyager.

In conclusion, studying and understanding your family is the necessary intermediate step for understanding transactions between you and the world outside. It allows you to look inside yourself and outside at the environment with a new cohesive perspective. In knowing the pathways through which events affected your parents and affect you in your emotional world, you arrive at a new awareness of the context in which you live.

XI

⎯⎯⎯⎯⎯ ⟡ ⎯⎯⎯⎯⎯

DISINTEGRATING
FAMILIES—1: DIVORCE

MORE AND MORE the marriages we make are not good enough for us. Our families are being broken apart, not by external circumstances but by choice, and the United States has the highest divorce rate in the Western world. Last year there were approximately two million marriages and one million divorces. The chance for some kind of prolonged marital separation for couples is probably around 50 percent; for divorce in middle-aged couples or younger, 35 to 40 percent. The divorce and separation rate is rising even more rapidly in families with children than in marriages as a whole, and one out of three children under eighteen years of age does not live with his or her two natural parents. One out of six lives with one parent. More important than statistics, divorce is now a norm, "par for the course," in certain places and age groups. Marriage holds us back, we seem to think. We see *it* and our mates as the problem, not ourselves. How should we cope with these changes—the phenomena of rising divorce rates and the increasing number of fragmented or part families?

Divorce is on the increase because what people want in their lives and the way they view marriage have changed. In a society

where career or self-fulfillment is prized to the exclusion of everything else, marriage and family life must adjust to the needs of
ambitious working people who believe that marriage obstructs
not only productivity but freedom and "growth" as well. For a
whole new generation of Americans there is a new hedonism,
a pursuit of pleasure, a "living for the moment" orientation. This
pleasure principle is probably the result of the depressing emotional tone that the current generation observed in their parents
as they were growing up. People who are middle-aged now can
remember the pervasive sense of unending helplessness in the face
of economic or military threat. Because people naturally identify
with their parents in the past and their children in the present,
current ideas about parenthood had roots in the Depression and
in World War II. Those who wished, in the thirties and forties, to
unburden their parents and give them pleasure identify with them
now, "let it all hang out" in their own lives, and release their own
children from too much closeness and what they perceive as a
burden of guilt. Others who lost their parents to war or poverty
search for them in success, pleasure, and a variety of marital partners. In either case, whether the obligation to family was oppressive and resented or wholly absent, modern adults, because of
unresolved emotional issues with their own parents and their own
past, are very likely to abandon their families and the children
in them. The elimination of legal, economic, and moral barriers
against divorce is the result rather than the cause of our attitude
as a society toward the family.

There are different kinds of divorces just as there are different
kinds of marriages. To understand the wish to separate from the
spouse we must examine the kind of intimate relationship the
husband and wife had, and the personality of each. We must know
the early family history, the development and early relationships
of each member of the couple, the ideas and example of marriage
in and around the family, and in the mind of each parent, and
each spouse's experience with separation early in life.

THE FIRST IMPORTANT EXPERIENCE of separation is the "psychological birth of the human infant," as termed by Drs. Margaret

Mahler, Fred Pine, and Anni Bergman, in the first year or two of life, when there is a growing awareness of separateness from the mother figure. It is a crucial time for future relationships. The child modulates his feelings toward his parents, develops a sense of his own identity, learns what thoughts can do and what they cannot do, and learns how his behavior affects others. He learns who produces what, uses certain people and avoids others, and comes to know the difference between his perceptions and the reality around him. Most important, he learns that all of his expectations will not be fulfilled and he adjusts his behavior accordingly. At this time he is assembling and learning to use his most basic psychological equipment for relationships, and the expectations he is left with, while usually still out of his conscious awareness, are the ones that determine his ability to relate to intimates later on.

In infancy there is one parental figure—let us call her the mother—who gives care and pleasure to the child, and there is another parental figure—let us call him the father—who limits gratification and provides frustration so that the child builds "emotional muscles" and grows.

After separation from the mother figure, the most important period, as far as its later impact on marriage is concerned, is four to six years of age. The child has a full-blown love affair with the parent of the opposite sex, which includes sexual fantasies—for instance, "having Daddy's baby" or "giving Mommy a baby." We can see these wishes in children of this age group, in their play and in how they relate to their parents and parent figures. (They wish to possess one parent and get rid of the other, their rival.) The frustration and resolution of these wishes are what lead to sexual identity and a desire for union with another after adolescence.

Adolescents have lots of fantasies and sexual urges, and usually a wish to find someone with whom they can live, marry, and make a family. At the end of adolescence one of two things usually happens to people. First, they can "fall in love." Love is very much a motivation for marriage, especially in American society. Second, they can choose someone from a limited number of eligibles, based on geographical area, age, race, religion, personality, education, and other characteristics, and the testing process known as dating, or courtship, begins. A friendship develops which can turn into love after an hour or after a number of years.

Dr. Henry Dicks, the English psychiatrist, and Dr. James Framo, the family therapist, have written most definitively about marriage. Consciously, people marry for a sense of belonging, to satisfy creature comforts, to attain a "family feeling," and for sex (even in today's world of sexual liberation, there are those who desire sex in the context of an emotionally intimate relationship). There are those who wish to avoid loneliness and want a companion or competitor or scorekeeper or sparring partner. Others wish to have children and through them become immortal. While these are the usual conscious reasons, unconscious, potentially irrational, forces are always more powerful in marriages.

The whole process from "eligibility" to "relationship" to "love" is determined by earlier experience, and goes on in the conscious and the unconscious mind together. People "fall in love" on the basis of particular physical features which conform to an image or fantasy deep within themselves. A young Jewish man, for instance, can choose to marry in his faith, or for reasons outside of his awareness, he may be able to love only non-Jewish women (the *shiksa* cheerleader syndrome). There are women who in the course of three or four marriages marry only Navy men or vodka drinkers or men with mustaches, without knowing why. When it comes to love—that state of mixed yearning, bliss, and obsession—external circumstances and internal unconscious factors are constantly intertwined. Can anyone doubt the impossibility of the love between Romeo and Juliet or the inevitability of the love on the desert island in *Swept Away*?

Freud felt that the roots of love lay in old feelings toward a parent or toward one's own self-image. A man might love a woman who in some way triggers off an old feeling he had toward a mother figure who cared for him; a woman's love might relate to feelings toward a father figure who protected her. Love can also arise from feelings or wishes about oneself which a loved one represents or helps satisfy, an idealized image of what one might have been in the past or might want to be in the present or future.

Love is blind to the real other person because it has less to do with him or her than it has to do with the self and one's past. There is a type or look or characteristic of a loved person that stirs up these old deep feelings from the unconscious, and the wish is for permanent possession of the other person, the embodiment of these feelings.

BEFORE, DURING, AFTER, or instead of love there is another process going on in marital relationships in which one is a bit less blind to the real characteristics of the other person. An interchange occurs. Each partner tests and molds the other on an intense one-to-one basis, as well as in a variety of social situations. It is a twenty-four-hour-a-day unconscious negotiation process. It involves old feelings from one's first experience of intimacy with parents, and includes unfinished emotional business with one or another parent, old "sore points" and fears of various kinds. In short, in the new intimate relationship old identities emerge and partners become more and more the way they were as infants and children. The old feelings that emerge are varied and can involve just about any wish or emotion. For instance, a wish for constant loving or attention, a wish for power, perfection, protection, or consolation; rage or fear toward men or women, just about everything and anything that one can carry as an emotional residue from early experience. One or another kind of feeling emerges in just about everyone, but these feelings become problems only when they are rigid, constant, and interfere with other aspects of the relationship. There is between the two parties a "fit" with more or less tension or satisfaction, and the style of relating becomes increasingly automatic and comfortable for each.

Courtship, like a honeymoon, becomes a blissful state where the possession of the loved one solves all the old emotional problems and makes everything right. There is a promise of gratification of all the old wishes and protection from all the old fears, a fantasy of "eating the cake and having it too."

In the early marital relationship, when people feel they belong to each other, like parents and children belong to each other, each one finds in the other the pleasure-giving and simultaneously frustrating loved one, a kind of mother and father in the spouse.

The wish for either figure changes over time. Most commonly, men relate as they would to a mother figure, women to a father figure, early in marriage. Later on, however, men can complain that their wives are inefficient. They want a chum, someone to be dependable, to share activities, even masculine activities with. Women later on want more tenderness, warmth, and understanding. It is the need for the parent of the same sex emerging from repression, usually as a response to having children.

Spouses play different roles for each other, according to the events in the family life cycle, and since they play some better than others, marital tension rises and falls accordingly.

SOONER OR LATER, there is disappointment that the partner does not provide the solutions to all the old problems and wishes, and in fact does not play the expected role as constantly as one desires. There is a mutuality to this expectation, and spouses tend to punish each other by disappointing the other as they feel disappointed themselves. All marriages are at one time or another a "mutual disappointment society." There is working and reworking to make a fit with one's mate, as a way of handling one's inner feelings. One hears about the marriage problems ("She's careless"; He's insensitive"; "She's a nag"; "He's cold"), but the feelings underneath come from within the self. They arise really as a response to events outside the marriage, or from deep inside, from roots in one's own past history. They occur in all marriages and continue throughout the family cycle in accordance with events. The more aware one is, emotionally as well as intellectually, of the origins of these feelings within the self, the less one invokes the partner as the cause of one's misery when it occurs, and the more one sees him or her as a real person and can use him or her as a source of support.

These unconscious aspects of the marriage contract are felt rather than known, or are at the fringes of awareness and come up in fantasies, dreams and complaints about the spouse that do not seem to fit and do not seem to change as the spouse changes. Each partner has his own contract and even seems to feel, although he may superficially know otherwise, that the partner knows the contract but simply does not fulfill his part of the bargain. Feelings of rage, disappointment, hurt, and vulnerability are important in setting the emotional tone of the family. In truth, partners can be quite surprised at the other's expectation of them.

Each event in the family life cycle, including everyday events such as sex, pregnancy, fertility, infertility, the birth of a child, the first daughter, a second son, success, sickness, all trigger feelings in each spouse that are worked through in the relationship with the other. All things are mediated through the marriage. To the extent that there is tension, there is blame for one's partner or depression in oneself.

HOW DOES MARITAL tension relate to divorce? When does dissatisfaction lead to separation and what are the consequences for family members? Formation of "part families" is not new. Families are built to handle separation, loss, and even violence. What is new is the domestic form such violence takes, its effect on emotional healing processes and subsequent family functioning.

We have seen that the roots of marital tension and conflict are deep within the individual personality and we know that dissatisfaction does not always lead to divorce. As Dr. Framo puts it, divorce is an "attempt to solve an internal problem by external means."

Divorce is a choice, a pathway more or less open, sometimes even inevitable, depending upon the history of divorce or separation in a spouse's family of origin. There can be marital dissatisfaction without divorce and divorce without dissatisfaction. There can be a sudden desire to free oneself of family responsibility, which can become stifling in response to turning thirty or forty or fifty, or to losing a certain status or job or parent. It can be a reaction to change in a spouse or child, real or imagined.

Divorce occurs in a vulnerable but sometimes stable marriage, usually activated by one partner and fought by the other, whose surprise can be quite genuine. A course of events is set in motion against the divorce because the family is an ongoing system which tends to resist change. The desire for separation is not necessarily a repudiation of the family as an institution, since divorced people usually remarry. Sometimes it is a wish to do something to a particular member: to hurt, to reject, also to free or protect a spouse or a child. With its tendency to maintain itself, and to keep in balance, the family system changes dramatically. Each member adopts a different stance toward each of the others. Rival children can become allies, parents in their anger and depression become closer, more sensitive and tied to each other. Sometimes these changes in family structure are enough to abort the divorce.

The family becomes like a group of people throwing a life line to a member in a stormy sea. Although marriage can precipitate emotional difficulty because it fosters the re-emergence of old, infant, and childhood feelings in the new relationship, once it is entered into, marriage secures a person against emotional stress. It allows one to use the partner as an object for those old troublesome feelings, keeping them in check. One functions better outside because of the marriage. A wish to jump the family ship when the voyage gets rough is a threat to all members and stimulates the natural protective forces of the family.

If the threat of separation is not resolved by a return to the old equilibrium or the establishment of a new one, the divorce process is set in motion. The family becomes a stress environment. Tension increases, usually with depression. Individuals are turned inward toward the family and toward themselves. Adults cannot concentrate so well at work. Children do poorly in school. There is irritability, blame, and an active fantasy life, especially in children, of rescuing or of reuniting the parents. The roles—who acts and who is acted upon—are rigid. Because both parties are ambivalent, each at times questioning or changing his or her mind in fantasy, there is heightened anxiety with any real changing of the roles. If the divorcing partner changes his mind, he or she is told, "Make up your mind; what do you want anyway?" If the passive partner who resisted the divorce thinks it might not be a bad idea after all, especially because it is not his fault, since he is not the one initiating it, his partner can literally explode with anxiety at the prospect of losing control. Confusion only brings false hope, and the turning point in the process seems to be the change in how the family presents itself to outsiders.

A small number of marriages seem to be binding in only a small degree, arrangements for partners who function frequently without the other. For the most part, however, divorce is deeply traumatic for all family members. Two people who chose each other, lived with each other, solved problems and had children together, see, hear, and smell each other every day for years, become connected on the deepest levels of human existence. The automatic way in which they use each other emotionally in marriage—the resiliency, the emotional strength in reserve—usually makes divorce a crisis for everyone concerned. To rip, or be ripped away from, this interpersonal system affects every individual in the field. Other family members hate, reject, or cling to one another. Psychiatrists call it "retaliatory separation" or "identification with the lost object" or person. For systems theorists it is like throwing a magnet into a precisely modulated electromagnetic field. Each individual's connection with the separating spouse or parent has turned out to be a source of pain. Children feel that the primary rule of sticking by one another has been broken, the foundation of the family crushed. Children always become pawns. They volunteer themselves in this regard. Everyone changes. Quiet, sympathetic, loving women wish their husbands dead, preferring amputation over chronic social and emotional disease. Honorable men strike their wives and talk about them with words that would embarrass prostitutes. It is no wonder that such a high percentage of murders are committed within the family, that policemen are cautious and even terrified when called to handle domestic conflict. In the unconscious and in the family, separation equals psychological death.

In addition to rage, there is guilt and depression. One partner can cling, the other can feel suffocated. A male-hating, "castrating" woman can reject her husband, now reduced to helplessness and dependency; it is the fulfillment of a much earlier wish, usually not even remembered, to do the same thing to a rejecting father. A "male chauvinist" can reject a woman for the same reason he married her years earlier, her femininity now having become uninteresting, a sign of "passivity." There is frequently a cycle of accommodation, second chances, and exhaustion. Both partners lose self-esteem, believing the other's accusations, feeling guilty, not only because of their rage but because of their failure in the marriage. The fictions, dreams, and plans of the marital pair and family crumble away. Honesty has undesired effects, sending a desired spouse further away, or making a dependent one cling more, and the conflict only increases. An atmosphere of terror, depression, and uncertainty develops for the children, who grasp for information to divert them from their fantasies.

The process is one that is similar to mourning, in that it probably cannot be shortened and must be assimilated piecemeal, each memory, hope and pleasure relinquished one at a time.

Death is often easier than divorce for family members because there is less of a feeling of responsibility, less decision making, and less daily stress in the situation. Emotionally, divorce is like loss of a parent. It leaves one helpless. In fact, many divorces are precipitated by death or decline of a spouse's parent. People feel old, alone, and mortal when a parent dies and can divert themselves by blaming their marriage. Really, it is a wish to punish or desert the spouse in the way one feels punished or deserted by the parent, a kind of retaliatory separation.

Anger, bitterness, and self-justification are probably necessary ingredients for divorce for a period of time.

After separation, there are a number of possibilities. A person can become a family satellite, leaving the family but staying attached emotionally. Men and women do this to maintain a family feeling, to show they have done "their duty" as citizens, or even to forestall other relationships. At other times, anger and a desire for vengeance are maintained, and as long as these feelings are alive, there is no true separation. This kind of rage can persist even though people are divorced and remarried. Second husbands and wives are spared the angry side of the mate, yet they are also denied a full emotional relationship.

Ideally, one comes to perceive the divorced partner as just another person, and then one becomes emotionally available to another relationship. Most divorced persons remarry and their second marriages are almost as durable as first marriages. This is not true, however, of third and fourth marriages. When remarriages do fail, one frequently hears complaints about the new spouse identical to or sometimes opposite to the complaints heard in the first marriage. Those who are most free of a previous marital relationship say that there were some good times and some bad times, and they appreciate the growth within themselves. If parents can allow themselves to be free of their spouses, if they can accept themselves, they are not compelled to shatter the residual family structure and the children who need it. They can let go of the past and take a chance on the future.

Individuals going through a divorce must move away from depression and limitless anger at the spouse. They must learn how and why they brought separation about, or if they think *they* do not want separation but the partner does, then they should work on what separation means and *could* mean for them. The most important "mooring" anyone has is the family, the very thing that seems to be unavailable. But the family does not really disintegrate. It changes. The idea of the family—the loyalty, the identity that spouses have—endures. So do the parenting role, the community, and the family of origin.

The most important rule for spouses in the crisis of divorce is to be with others, especially their family of origin, yet they must be with them in a constructive rather than destructive way. Attachment to a family of origin can be a cause for problems in a marriage. And a divorced parent is almost inevitably thrown back into a kind of adolescence.

But if one can be together without being emotionally entangled with one's original family, redoing, if necessary, the separation work of adolescence, one can emerge as a better parent and a more mature husband or wife in the future.

We have seen that the roots of marital tension and conflict lie deep within the individual personality. We know, also, that all the things that happen to people from within the family life cycle and from the world outside are somehow mediated through the family, especially the marriage.

But marital tension and even dissatisfaction do not always lead to divorce. Rather, divorce depends upon family factors, divorce in the family history and separation early in life, as well as social factors: the spouses' work, peer group, mobility pattern and expectations.

If you are going through a divorce, you can increase emotional stability and aid the healing process after separation by learning about yourself and your family. The more you focus on yourself rather than the spouse (your own feelings and why you have them, your own goals and why they cannot be fulfilled in the marriage), and the less you focus outside the self (blaming the spouse or family or job), the more prepared you will be for divorce.

Divorce can be a mindless act to avoid growth. At other times it can be the end of one relationship and a move on to a better one. It is usually a crisis for the spouses and an emotional disaster for children. "Crisis" implies danger, but it does not *necessarily* imply damage to adults or children. You can minimize the destructive effects of divorce by knowing yourself, your place in your life cycle and your family's place in its cycle. You can also be with others, not only in a family of origin but in a group or in an organization of any kind, by working or volunteering. If you can be with your former spouse and even in-laws (very difficult at first) involved with the parenting function and with that function only, you have probably worked through the separation.

You should *attend* your divorce proceedings. You should refuse to feel victorious or defeated in this increasingly common life event. Gradually, with these approaches, you can work out your feelings the way you choose to, with changes in your lifestyle, activities, and image rather than with repression of anger and displacement onto children.

CHILDREN OF DIVORCE

INCREDIBLE AS IT SEEMS, with the millions spent on medical and psychiatric research, with the reams of publications, reports and books on marriage, there are fewer than a dozen recent articles with a scientific approach on the effects of divorce on children. In a general way, these few reports confirm that the effects vary according to the age of the child and the family situation before and after the separation.

One of the two most noteworthy is a study by Judith S. Wallerstein and Joan B. Kelly of sixty divorced families in Marin County, California. The results have been printed in a series of articles called the "Children of Divorce Project." Children and parents were interviewed at the time of divorce and then again one year later to observe emotional effects like depression, anxiety, withdrawal, and poor functioning. The word most frequently used to describe the results is "sobering." The younger the child, the more severe were the effects. This is understandable, since the family supposedly secures the child from loss or harm from the outside, and the younger he is, the more he depends on it for protection.

These children suffered an acute crisis related to loss of a parent and the turmoil of divorce, as well as long-term emotional problems that appeared later on.

The two-and-a-half- to three-and-a-half-year-old group experienced regression in toilet training, irritability, whining, crying, fearfulness, separation anxieties, sleep problems, confusion, aggressiveness, and tantrums. It was noted that these symptoms occurred in children all but one of whom remained with their mother in their same home environment. Their play was "joyless." In play therapy interviews, they constructed unsafe worlds inhabited by dangerous animals, and they told stories of "woebegone searching." They were confused and frightened. Three out of nine in this age group were more troubled a year after the divorce, and it was learned that these three came from a home where the divorce conflict persisted and mothers were preoccupied much of the time.

The four-year-olds were also severely depressed, confused, and blamed themselves for the divorce. Seven out of eleven were more depressed, more constricted in play and behavior, and expressed a greater need for approval, attention, and physical contact after the divorce. This occurred despite more loving contact and what *seemed* to be a better relationship with father on visits than existed before the divorce. It seemed to relate to a change in the mother, her preoccupation with affairs, and her attempts to move into the father's role.

A total of 44 percent of these preschool children were more emotionally upset one year after the divorce than they were before. The most important correlation was the emotional availability of the mother and the quality of the child's relationship with her.

The five- and six-year-olds presented for the first time children who could handle divorce between their parents. Girls seemed more vulnerable at this age to loss of their fathers, and they maintained sad fantasies of recovering their fathers with their love. Visitations were almost like courtship with disappointment after they were over. The girls seemed preoccupied with their fantasies and functioned poorly at school.

Fifty percent of the five- and six-year-old children seemed able to handle the divorce crisis, and 25 to 50 percent remained sad, fearful, confused about loyalties and yearned for their fathers. Visiting was not enough for them, except when they could visit at will and such a pattern was approved of by both parents. This is consistent with the view that the child like everyone else in the family must emotionally work through the old relationship with the father who has been lost, and work out something new. The child compares the image of the father born of old memories and feelings with the real father in front of him. It is a kind of grieving reaction for the old relationship, it takes time, and it depends upon a stable availability. In children of this age the "divorce event" was less important than the "divorce process," the changes occurring over the course of *several years* to the children in these families.

Older children and adolescents were often able to handle divorce between their parents without significant emotional effects. They could understand the situations, feel and express anger, and if they were old enough, could distance themselves from the difficulties of their parents. In fact, the more distant and uninvolved they were, the more capable they were in handling the divorce. They then seemed to be able to resist attempts by parents to engage them as allies or chums. In a systems sense, divorce breaks a family alliance between mother and father, and there is a pressure for alliance between the parent and the adolescent, undercutting the normal generation boundary between parent and child. The stress brings a desire in the mother for closeness with her child. Becoming "pals" with a parent, however, does not work so well. The child feels the loss of mother in addition to the loss of father rather than the creation of a friend. In other words, the more distant and even cold the adolescent appears, the more stable is the family structure and the better the young person seems to perform.

Overall, the findings in this study where 25 to 50 percent of children of divorce remain seriously affected in their mood, functioning, and development, are staggering when one considers that between nine and eighteen million children in this country live in families where divorce or separation has taken place. Moreover, the length of time they are affected, the poignancy of their perceptions and fantasies, the absence until recently of any moral or psychological standards for their experience make the situation of these "Children of Armageddon" one of the most urgent issues for our time.

XII

DISINTEGRATING FAMILIES—2: THE NEED FOR CHILD-CUSTODY REFORM

> Someday, maybe, there will exist a well-informed,
> well-considered, and yet fervent public conviction that the most
> deadly of all possible sins is the mutilation of a child's spirit.
>
> ERIK ERIKSON

WHEN MARRIAGE was a sacrament, when people were married in the eyes of God, bound by a powerful legal document, "together through sickness and health 'til death do you part," they acted for others: spouses, children, and society. People in unhappy marriages often stayed together "for the sake of the children." Spouses viewed each other the way children viewed their parents. Children do not choose their parents or siblings. They come to understand and expect that family members belong to one another, and that is that.

Formerly, when divorce occurred it was somebody's "fault." There was an aggressor and an aggrieved—someone deserted or was cruel or adulterous, and children usually went to that parent who was aggrieved, or to the one who at least had the better case in law.

Beginning with a court decision in this country in 1887, the "best interests of the child" became an important consideration for custody awards. It was modeled after the sixteenth-century English doctrine of *Parens Patriae*, which held that the state should protect and become "parent" for those who do not have protectors, including children of divorcing parents. To simplify matters, the "best interests of the child" usually coincided with parental morality, and custody went to the morally upright (and legally prepared) parent, in most cases the man. Father represented the family and was responsible for it. Divorce was unusual, a stigma, an adversary proceeding, with one person guilty and the other innocent or at least less guilty.

After World War II, with the growth of the movement for self-fulfillment and its emphasis on the primacy of pleasure, when pleasure became something literally to "pursue," the divorce rate increased in this country as people felt less compunction about ending marriages which were unsatisfactory or personally limiting. Many said that children were better off in a home without conflict than in one where there were arguments, stress, and marital unhappiness. This was true if the result of divorce was a one-parent family. It was especially true if there was another "father figure or mother figure" around to provide a model for children growing up in the household. One father seemed as good as another. As usual, the prevalent beliefs concerning children of divorce conveniently matched the wishes of parents and the fashion of the times.

Nowadays, child-custody cases are neither as unusual or as simple as they used to be. Despite the new hedonism and the small but increasing number of divorce cases where neither spouse wants the children, custody still constitutes one of the most important issues of divorce. About 60 to 70 percent of divorces involve minor children, over one million of them a year, and in many of these cases, even those that are eventually settled, there are prolonged legal contests lasting up to two years, usually concerning money or children. Custody battles are part of the "post-divorce turbulence" that Dr. Jack Westman describes: spouses remain dedicated to each other, usually with hate, sometimes with hopes of reunion, and use children to fight each other.

There has also been a growing awareness that courts have been ineffective in determining the "best interests of the child."

As Robert H. Mnookin, director of the Childhood and Government Project, University of California, put it: "Despite the agony of well-meaning judges . . . the judicial process evokes dis-satisfaction, and frequently outrage, from those who have studied the performance of our courts in custody disputes. Delay, ar-bitrariness, and unpredictability earmark the conduct of these proceedings. Under the rubric of determining "the best interests of the child," trial judges have largely unreviewable discretion to decide custody cases according to their own typically unarticu-lated values and hunches."*

Courts fail to understand the psychological needs of children, especially children of divorce. The presumption is that the court should decide child custody, with the usual criterion "the best interests of the child," because children are helpless, dependent, and are not a part of the adversary divorce proceeding. Perhaps there is also a notion, somewhere in this, that the parents are *not* concerned with the best interests of the child, that they are inter-ested in winning in court. There may even be a notion that if they really cared about the children, they would not divorce at all. For this reason the court looks out for the child and decides which parent is more "fit." The "Child's Bill of Rights," a recent docu-ment drawn up by a group of child advocates, includes the right to "child-centered" divorce and custody laws.

In unresolved cases, judges usually evaluate the parents, trying to distinguish between those character faults that affect the chil-dren and the capacity to be a parent, and those that do not. Fit-ness determinations vary with the times, the community, and the particular judge. At one time, adultery was tantamount to "unfit-ness." In the current age of "sexual enlightenment," this is un-usual. The enlightenment does not go very far, however. Drug use, other than alcohol, for instance, does not seem to the courts to be consistent with fitness as a parent. Alcohol use probably varies with the area of the country, the judge's view, and perhaps even his own drinking pattern.

One of the most common barbarisms of the system are the "meetings in chambers" where the judge will see children, pre-sumably to get the true story. He wants to hear the wishes of each

---

* *Journal of Child Psychiatry*, Vol. XIV, No. 1 (Winter 1975), page 180, "Book Reviews."

child. There are times it also seems that he wants to satisfy his own curiosity, even to see and hear and perhaps hold the child over whom there is such a struggle. For the child, the terror of rehearsal for an interview in chambers and the dread of cross-examination afterward by one or both parents are nothing compared to his fantasies. He worries about his performance in this procedure, which seems to cause such anxiety in his parents even as they say, "He's a nice old man. He has a nice leather chair." It is the performance of the child's life, a contest to see which parent can terrorize him more, an empty gesture which demands everything from the child and offers half an hour of phony inversion of the power structure; thirty minutes for the child to manipulate rather than be manipulated. This ritual, usually useless and sometimes cruel, of seeing this "part family" in an artificial environment, is an exercise in terror, akin in medicine perhaps to a pre-operation run-through before the amputation of an arm or leg.

Professionals who are responsible for these decisions and take this child-oriented approach are frequently emotionally involved. They become "child savers" and burden the children by offering what they themselves as adults would want—freedom of choice.

These children need parents, not liberty or equity. Again, it is a confusion of institutions between family and society. Hearings which threaten one or another parent threaten the children as well. One should never ask children to reject a parent. To do so is like asking children who are displaced by war to take sides in it. They must reject the parent, and to reject the parent is to reject the self.

People choose their mates; they do not choose their parents. Even in literature—for instance, in Dickens—when children are rescued by a benevolent parent figure, it happens by chance, not choice. When a child is given power over his parenting, he is no longer a child. He becomes depressed. He has no hope of recovering his parents because parents without authority are no parents at all. For children a sense of belonging, without choice, is the very foundation of the family. The child thinks that his own wishes and freedom of choice are what caused the divorce and turned his world upside down in the first place.

All of these situations are highly complex. When children do make a choice, it is usually a response to pressure by a parent. Or they may side with an apparent victor because of their own sense of terror and confusion. The "choice" may, in fact, reflect a stronger attachment to a preferred parent, or it may be a submission out of fear. Children perhaps can express anger at the parent whom they reject, while they may be inhibited toward the parent whom they "choose." They may simply be acting out of self-preservation in a terrifying, chaotic, and confusing situation.

For the child, interviews and declarations of preference are terrifying, a nightmare come true, the power of life and death (continuity or separation) over the parent. They are also a first course in manipulation, an expression of anger to avoid depression, a new way of mishandling, avoiding, and relabeling feelings that can become the pattern for a lifetime. When the court refuses to see children, on the other hand, or to hear very much about their "welfare," it encourages parents to leave their children alone to work on resolving their own arrangements. Responsible adults should not solicit and should usually ignore expressions of loyalty and preference from such confused, abused, and overburdened children.

The problem goes beyond the courts, however, and says something about our value system as a society. Administered by well-meaning but fallible judges, whose ability varies according to the degree of corruption or enlightenment in the local area, the domestic-relations courts are the "minor leagues" of any judiciary. Important cases in our society concern (1) money—corporate law, taxes, antitrust litigation; and (2) newsmaking cases involving crimes or radical politics. Those few talented and diligent family-court judges interested in domestic-relations law itself, in addition to its application in their courts, are incredibly overworked because there are just too many cases involving troubled families for them to handle. Often they throw up their hands and quit. There is also a tendency, an extremely misguided one, to choose individuals who seem to have "empathy" as judges in family courts. This quality is often not empathy at all but inadequacy, emotional vulnerability, a sensitivity to one's own feeling state that too frequently makes the judge uncomfortable. He wants to "calm things down." In front of a raging husband and a tearful wife often as old as his own wife or child, in a case which requires the wisdom of King Solomon, he delays decision and really would like to be out of the courtroom as quickly as possible. His "hidden agenda" becomes one of delay and escape. Cases go on interminably with report after report, interview after interview. The result can be rationalized. "Maybe they'll resolve this thing themselves."

The whole issue of how a professional's own feelings are stirred up by a work situation and interfere with his effectiveness is known in psychiatry as "counter-transference." Counter-transference issues are perhaps the most important, most repetitive and reworked issues in any good psychiatric training program, especially if it is psychoanalytically oriented. Major amounts of supervision time can be spent on the subtleties of how the psychiatrist's or the psychoanalyst's own feeling state is being affected by the patient and the situation before him. This is the reason why psychiatrists and other professionals frequently undergo psychoanalysis or therapy themselves, to understand how their personalities and past experiences affect their functioning.

Although they rely on mental-health experts, judges are not and need not be trained as mental-health professionals. The problem is that flexibility, latitude, and "compassion" born of ambivalence in hearing family cases too often increase the chance for ineffectiveness in court. It is probably the misunderstood *Parens Patriae* doctrine, the secondary status of these courts in our society, and the law itself that should be changed.

Human injustice is less important and less interesting to us than financial or criminal injustice. We make few demands of these courts. We ignore them except when there are famous people or newsworthy crimes involved, or in rare instances, when they concern adoption cases which intrigue us. Our judges are chosen politically, and the courts that matter least and have no importance for those who choose and assign judges are the family courts. They are "equity courts," which give judges lots of flexibility and "latitude" for decisions, and incompetence is difficult to prove. Such a judgeship is the ideal reward for someone a political party wants to get rid of in a friendly way.

With incompetent lawyers and failed politicians whose only

attribute is loyalty to the party deciding cases, justice is blind, deaf, and dumb in domestic relations courts. The system serves political, not social issues, and society fails its families.

Granted these cases are difficult; still, many of the decisions are nothing short of horrendous. When one reads them one finds an incredible disparity in the degree of sophistication in different parts of the country. Some judges seem to be sensitive, insightful, emotionally mature. Others seem to be inadequate, inconsistent, and volatile persons who can be placed in these courts because no one cares what happens in them.

The law itself can be as ridiculous as the court system. For instance, the monumental absurdity of having different jurisdictions, each making different custody rulings based on flimsy residence requirements, denies the simple reality that children are more the citizens of their families than of any state or jurisdiction. It invites parents to disrupt their families and move somewhere else when they are less than totally satisfied with a court ruling. Child stealing, leaving a jurisdiction when one is dissatisfied with a court ruling, destroys families, spouses, and children, and is not even a crime, partly because it reflects contempt for a contemptible court system. Children are not merely pawns in these situations, they are self-sacrificing weapons used in the service of extortion or the sad destruction of one spouse by another. There are a number of communities in the United States and the Caribbean where divorce and child-custody cases seem to be a major industry, all because of our weak, antiquated domestic relations law and its application by ambivalent judges, an inadequate judiciary, and the society behind it.

In any case, popular "enlightened" rules of thumb until recently for child-custody cases have included (1) a young child should be with the mother; (2) a girl should be with her mother, while a boy should be with his father as long as he no longer requires his mother's constant care; (3) the child's wishes should be taken into account; (4) there should be visitation rights for the parent not having custody; (5) children, wherever possible, should be with their biological parents; (6) if there are no questions of custody or physical abuse, society should not be involved in determining the best interests of the child or fitness of parents.

Mental-health professionals have recently undertaken efforts to help judges faced with the task of determining the "best interests of the child." Some psychiatrists simply accept the law for what it is and try to help however they can in specific cases. Others believe the law is right, that the child's interests should properly be the most important factor in deciding custody cases. Joseph Goldstein, Anna Freud, and Albert Solnit in *Beyond the Best Interests of the Child* agree that such an approach will break "the cycle of grossly inadequate parent-child relationships." With this as society's stated goal in these cases, children will be served better and become better parents. In this important book, these authors give some valuable information. They point out the ways in which children differ from adults.

Children have less tolerance for frustration, an "intense sensitivity to the length of separations," and an "egocentric" perspective that allows them to perceive events as occurring only for themselves. They can experience moving as a "grievous loss imposed on them; the birth of a sibling as an act of parental hostility"; illness or distraction of a parent as rejection, separation as an abandonment or punishment for their thoughts or feelings. A child's ability to *hear* "Mommy and Daddy are separating because they don't love each other; it has nothing to do with you" depends on the child's age more than the intentions or enlightenment of his parents. With little ability to predict things, with a limited knowledge of the world and of themselves, the child experiences intense anxiety and feelings of helplessness with any separation. The younger the child, the less he can tolerate such frustration.

In being cared for physically and emotionally, infants and children develop a relationship with a particular person on whom they depend. The child needs a continuity of this relationship more than he needs anything else. It stabilizes the process of identification by which he grows, and according to these authors, his tie to this particular individual who functions as his "psychological parent" should be protected, satisfying each child's need for continuity. In custody conflicts, therefore, children should go with their psychological parent or with the individual who is most capable of loving the child and making him feel a "wanted child," meeting his needs over time. Perhaps the most difficult situations

of all are those where one parent represents the current psychological parent, and the other the parent with the greater emotional
capability. In all cases, courts should make these decisions with
promptness and finality. What is due process for adults is an end-
less nightmare for children. Because the child perceives time
differently, the urgency for custody cases should match that of
medical emergencies requiring transfusions or operations which
demand court decisions immediately. For instance, children up to
two or three years of age react poorly and feel depressed when
parents are gone for more than a few days. Under five years of age,
two months is about the limit, while for older children it can be
stretched to six months or more.

Also, these three authors suggest that the custodial parent
should have full power to allow, restrict and arrange visitation
with a noncustodial parent, since children will "freely love more
than one adult" only if the individuals in question feel positively
towards one another. This idea may seem harsh, but it recognizes
the systems aspects of the parents-child triangle, the effect one
relationship has on another *relationship*. On a practical level,
harsh attitudes from professionals often push parents toward
greater flexibility. Finally, Goldstein, Freud, and Solnit wish to
safeguard the right of parents to raise their children as they see fit,
free of government intrusion except in cases of neglect and abandonment. There is an inconsistency with other modern experts,
however, who advocate a "Child's Bill of Rights" with increased
responsibility (and presumably intrusiveness), while these authors recommend "privacy." Recent thinking therefore has (1)
expanded the "best interests of the child" doctrine into a comprehensive "child's rights" program and (2) taken ideas about fitness
of parents from a moral dimension to a psychological one concerning emotional fitness for parenthood.

What constitutes fitness? The good parent is the one who meets
the child's needs and makes the child feel "wanted." Wanting the
child, as Goldstein, Freud, and Solnit describe it, is beneficial if it
is based not on a wish for possession for the parent's reasons, but
on a recognition of the "child's own personal characteristics."
There is in this the acknowledgment of the importance of the
contacts outside the relationship between the child and the psy-

chological parent. The child, for instance, may need a family or a family member in a way the custodial adult does not. Dr. Ivan Boszormenyi-Nagy, the family therapist, would make the acceptance by one parent of the child's need for his other parent the most important factor for determining fitness for custody. Whether judges are dilatory or diligent, however, "fitness" is difficult to define, and many cases drag on and on, often becoming a chronic disease for all involved.

A FAMILY SYSTEMS APPROACH

Kings 3, Chapter 3

16 Then came there two women, that were harlots, unto the king, and stood before him.

17 And the one woman said, O my lord, I and this woman dwell in one house; and I was delivered of a child with her in the house.

18 And it came to pass the third day after that I was delivered, that this woman was delivered also: and we *were* together; *there was* no stranger with us in the house, save we two in the house.

19 And this woman's child died in the night; because she overlaid it.

20 And she arose at midnight, and took my son from beside me, while thine handmaid slept, and laid it in her bosom and laid her dead child in my bosom.

21 And when I rose in the morning to give my child suck, behold, it was dead: but when I had considered it in the morning, behold, it was not my son, which I did bear.

22 And the other woman said, Nay; but the living *is* my son, and the dead *is* thy son. And this said, No; but the dead *is* thy son, and the living *is* my son. Thus they spake before the king.

23 Then said the king, The one saith, This *is* my son that liveth, and thy son *is* dead: and the other saith, Nay; but thy son *is* the dead, and my son *is* the living.

24 And the king said, Bring me a sword. And they brought a sword before the king.

25 And the king said, Divide the living child in two, and give half to the one, and half to the other.

26 Then spake the woman whose the living child *was* unto the king, for her bowels yearned upon her son, and she said, O my lord, give her

the living child, and in no wise slay it. But the other said, Let it be neither mine nor thine, *but* divide it.

27 Then the king answered and said, Give her the living child, and in no wise slay it: she *is* the mother thereof.

28 And all Israel heard of the judgment which the king had judged; and they feared the king: for they saw that the wisdom of God *was* in him, to do judgment.

IN THIS FIRST recorded family systems treatment case, King Solomon does a number of things dear to the hearts of modern family-crisis therapists. He acts promptly, deciding child custody in the first meeting. He uses nonverbal technique with himself as the agent of change, surprises all, and "reframes" the situation by doing the unexpected. In an instant, rage becomes fear and powerlessness for one of these women because of the King's position of power and the nature of the woman's attachment to the child. She is made to fear for the welfare of her offspring, and this fear is what King Solomon is looking for.

He enters the system, the triangle between the two women and the child, without losing his identity or sense of purpose. He is not emotionally entangled, and he is not a "rescuer." He is there to do justice. He learns the nature of the bonds between the parties by testing the mechanism of emotional release. He makes things explicit. He shows them what they are doing to the child, tearing him apart, by threatening to do it for them.

With this decision, King Solomon defines fitness for parenthood, the limits of human separability, and the role of society and of the professional in child-custody cases. For the "fit" mother, her child's welfare is more important than her wish for possession. She is even prepared to relinquish it for its own survival. There is a merging of personalities such that injury to the child is injury to the mother, an emotional unity that is more important than physical togetherness ("her bowels yearned upon her son"). For her, the child is a living thing with needs of its own. For the other woman, the child is property and could be divided.

In custody disputes, it should be recognized that a child is half one parent and half the other and is not divisible. The image and feeling of being torn apart is constantly with these children, except when there is no repudiation or devaluation of the spouse. Joan Kelly and Judith Wallerstein, the experts on the effects of divorce on children, quote a young boy who describes his parents' divorce with the following: ". . . 'it's splitting me in two.' To emphasize his dilemma, Robert threw his hand hatchet style down the middle of his forehead." Dr. E. James Anthony quotes another child: "I feel as if both my mother and father are inside me and are fighting, and then they are walking away from each other, breaking up my body so that I would go with them both, but if I did that, of course, I would die. I would be all broken up. I can only be a real live person if they join together again."

The parent who properly cares for the child recognizes the child's need for the two halves of himself. The fit parent is the one who allows the child to be with someone else when the child's welfare requires it, forever if necessary, with no preconditions. Tolerance for the child's visitation with the noncustodial parent is one way of applying this Biblical wisdom to modern custody cases.

The *Parens Patriae* doctrine is nowhere to be found in King Solomon's court. "Society" cannot be a parent. It is not a living thing. It cannot touch or love or give birth or parental care. Societies are not large families, just as families are not small societies. People live not in societies but in their families, two of them in dynamic equilibrium. One family, the one that is there in every person, is inside the self, in the feelings, images, and memories in our head and heart. The other is outside the self. Societies are artifacts, fictions, accretions of a group of families. They consist of people who act usually unknowingly on behalf of their own emotional needs, their own families, past and present.

Further, there is no concern in King Solomon's court for the "best interests of the child." Nowhere do we hear about compassion or concern for the child, or meetings in the "judge's chambers." King Solomon brings this aspect out of the parent. He does not compete as a parent, nor is he manipulated by his "concern" for the child, to side with or sympathize or care for the child, something he knows he cannot do. Instead, he strips power away from the women momentarily, challenges them, and brings out the mother's protectiveness, thus identifying her. King Solomon knows that the best way for society to care for its children is through their parents and families.

He recognizes the power almost of life and death that parents have over their children, takes it away until the true mother takes it back. She gives her infant life by sacrificing her wish for physical possession. The King decides custody on the basis of the mother's capacity to give for the sake of the child's welfare as she saw it. Parenthood *is* a sacrifice, and those in custody disputes, instead of discrediting the spouse and documenting their own fitness, might be challenged by the courts to focus their attention on what they will give up for the child's welfare.

With King Solomon's philosophy the courts would confront, challenge, and work with parents rather than replace them. The child in such situations needs to deal with the loss of an aspect of the parental system. Having as much as possible of both parents and the relationship that they have between each other, even if it is only tolerance, can minimize the trauma. Too often the loss of one parent is a loss of both. When the mother, if she is the custodial parent, becomes depressed or raging or tries to fill her husband's shoes, the child usually loses mother as well as father. The child can only do as well as the custodial parent, and more than anything else, the family needs support for her and her authority. Interestingly, whether the mother is employed outside the home is not a factor, but emotional availability is. Children with mothers who work fare better than those who do not, perhaps because of the mother's own increased sense of security.

Obviously, the loss can be minimized if there is visitation without conflict, a stable context as quickly as possible for working out feelings over the loss of the father, modulating the separation from him, and constructing a new kind of relationship with him with new expectations. The trend toward split custody, incidentally, where the child spends half the time with one parent and half the time with the other, is probably a positive one. It implies the preservation of a relationship with both parents, a changed rather than destroyed family structure, and a challenge that all can meet together. The chaos and confusion about arrangements are in the external world where they belong, an improvement over the usual situation where there is domestic neatness and inner turmoil or depression. Working hard at the difficult job of daily living, these families do what healthy families are supposed to do—stay in contact and accomplish tasks together. This arrangement should someday be routine in child-custody cases. The long, exhausting negotiation that is sometimes required can be an opportunity for growth. Often this is what parents need, to give up the marriage relationship and work out a new one as co-parents.

The criteria for determining fitness for child custody between contesting parents should be (1) tolerance for visitation; (2) ability to tolerate and communicate with the spouse (for instance, the ability to be in the presence of the spouse without undercutting his or her authority; the ability to focus strictly on issues of parenting without being engaged by other issues); (3) emotional stability in the custodial parent to deal with his or her own changes, to accept the authority of the court and the new reality for the family; and (4) a desire and an ability to resolve the case quickly according to the child's emotional needs, not a parent's legal or social needs, or the judge's calendar. Not only would these criteria define psychological parenting, they would encourage it. The *family* dimension should be the ethical one, and *society* should pressure spouses to become parents rather than litigants.

The criteria represent the parent's ability to see the child as a separate person with separate needs rather than as a possession or a prize of victory. Tolerance for visitation and for the spouse represent tolerance and respect for the family, for society, for one's own past, and for one's children and their future.

But all of these criteria should be demonstrated, not reported, either evoked by the court or observed in the "post-divorce turbulence" in the responses to past or proposed, temporary or permanent changes in the family system.

Judges should observe more and listen less, even though this is a difficult task when the record of a proceeding may become a reality for a second trial. Furthermore, they should forget about the "best interests of the child" and concentrate on serving justice.

Certain paradoxes emerge. Respect for the court and the sys-

tem, difficult when there is so little reason for it, is still an important sign of fitness because it is the beginning of control over
emotions and respect, or at least tolerance, for the spouse. Child
stealing, leaving a jurisdiction when the court does not do what
one wants, represents *unfitness*, a sign of the parent's inability to
accept authority, change, or the child's separateness, rather than a
demonstration of "love" for the child.

The parent who is successful in court may be the very one least
fit for parenting. In fact, court success may reflect unfitness more
clearly than anything else. Custody hearings, being the adversary
proceedings that they are, success in building a "good case," vilify-
ing and devaluing a spouse implies devaluation of the child. It
may indicate the way a person fails to deal with anger. Emotional
instability does not go together with good parenting, and attitudes
and treatment of a spouse reflect potential treatment of a child.
Rage at a spouse usually begins in previous rage at a parent, and
too often ends in abuse for a youngster.

Robert Mnookin asks why in our court system a child's welfare
should matter more than a parent's welfare, and this question
cuts to the heart of the matter. Dr. Nagy uses the term "multi-
lateral" for the approach that is crucial to apply in these cases. I
think "the best interests of the child" law makes us feel good about
ourselves. It serves *us*, not the families who are in court. It ennobles us, makes us "child savers." It allows us to punish parents
who do not "care" adequately. It is a comfortable slogan that
helps us, and the courts that represent us evade uncomfortable issues. It is only by forgetting the "best interests of the child" that
the court can better save the "best interests of the child." Rather
than punish parents, judges should protect them and safeguard
both parent-child relationships. By protecting parents they are
doing the *only* thing really within their power to help the children.
There is no way to separate "child's rights" from "parents' rights."
The "child-centered" divorce and custody laws that some advocate would probably create more cases in which we "abandon
children to their rights," as Dr. Solnit puts it, a phenomenon
professionals observe more and more frequently.

By remembering that the institution of parenthood is less
changeable than the institution of marriage, the court can be so-

ciety's representative, the true guardian of the eternal, immutable parts of the family structure. Society should preserve the family, changed though it may be. It should help parents preserve themselves, not "evaluate" them, or referee and judge the fight, and above all it should guarantee access from each part of the family system to the others. This "safe passage" not only includes children and parents but grandparents as well. Courts cannot dictate or even evaluate attachment. Rather, attachment *follows* from access to parents who are wholly available for interaction with the child. Courts *do* become part of the system, however, and *can* structure it so that natural healing processes will take place over time. But the courts must be clear about their task. Perhaps they should discourage the use of adversarial proceedings, and encourage the use of arbitration, counseling and *family* therapy, outside the courtroom. Inside the courtroom judges should be judges, not therapists, caretakers, or parents.

We need a uniform child-custody law that all the states and even nations can subscribe to. We need judges who are chosen not from the bottom of the political pork barrel but for their wisdom, training, and ability to handle emotional issues. We need new laws and new styles to our procedures to match the child's need for prompt contact with a caretaking parent, and the parent's need for gradual working through of the anger and depression that goes along with loss of a spouse. We need to take a long, hard look at the slogan "the best interests of the child" that is now the law, and what is produces. "The best interest of justice for all in the family" might be a better guiding principle, one that would help these individuals restructure their families. We should learn from those parents and children who have handled the divorce crisis well. We can then learn how to apply family systems theory and family science to this difficult area, and to all the other situations where children are not with parents.

We must work wherever possible to understand and decide domestic conflicts through family systems, not through temporary, part-families, by children in placement, or in judges' chambers. We must carry over this understanding and respect for the family into cases of foster care and adoption as well as into policy making for nurseries, day-care centers, medical care, and welfare-funding patterns. It is the family system inside and outside each person that is the indivisible, inseparable self that cannot be "torn asunder," and the implications for understanding this are enormous.

XIII

———— ◇ ————

ONE-PARENT FAMILIES
AND BLENDED FAMILIES

IN RECENT YEARS I have encountered more and more non-nuclear families, and the people in these situations have helped me develop new notions of what families are all about. The family is a multiplicity of institutions and processes: fatherhood, motherhood, parenthood, marriage, friendship, attachment, and detachment. The family takes many different forms to adapt to varied domestic situations. Our new configurations are stable groupings, not just transitional families. Today one out of three children does not live with his two natural parents. One out of six lives in a one-parent family.

There are three kinds of one-parent families: those where a parent, usually the father, has left or been left by his family, those where one parent has adopted a child, and those where an unmarried mother raises her children.

The history of the particular family, including the mythology that the history generates, is closely tied up with the special challenges that these families must face. If the family consists of a mother and her children, a task for all is to develop an attitude toward men that transcends the family's experience, which so frequently involves a male who has failed them.

Little boys can hate the maleness in themselves, learn to expect domination, protection, or constant adoration from women, or grow up and be forever obliged to protect a helpless mother. At other times they can feel overwhelmed, rebel against it, and run away from the family with its burdens and its sense of vulnerability at the earliest opportunity.

Little girls can grow up never able to trust or feel close to men. They have no model of what a relationship between a man and woman can be like. As teenagers, being younger, less vulnerable, and more desirable than mother can arouse guilt. They may get used to being miserable in their own adolescent and young adult lives. They can become too "independent" too soon and make a poor life decision about a husband-to-be just to leave the family.

For the group as a whole, the task is to develop a sense of security. Vulnerable to economic and physical danger, mother is easily overwhelmed and can become overprotective towards her children. Dependent on her own family and on social organizations, she hides feelings of envy and resentment toward others, including her children, whom she needs, or she feels odd—a failure in her domestic life. If there are others in her family or neighborhood in a similar plight, she feels better about herself, and support systems will be more acceptable to her.

Children are one step away from being orphans. Linked to each other, they inhibit aggressive feelings and forsake initiative because it often means going one's own separate way. They opt for security and togetherness to prevent depression, blame, and guilt from emerging in mother and in themselves. An oldest son or an only son can become a substitute father and single-handedly confront and overcome the family's real or fantasied vulnerability. More often, however, support systems like Big Brother organizations or other men in the extended family will respond and be available in times of stress as long as it is not too frequent and the approach is made according to the written and unwritten rules of the larger family group.

Fathers as the single parent with children also head a family which is incomplete, yet not necessarily unbalanced. Although the physical needs of the children and even the need for a mothering figure can be met, the female role and a model male-female relationship are lacking.

Again, the history of how the family came to be the way it is, as in all families, can reveal the challenges it must overcome. If the father is widowed, how long was he depressed and what happened to the family when he was? Is avoidance of depression structured into the family communication pattern? This kind of structure produces children with certain inhibitions. Loss of opportunities for fun, poor performance, and isolation from friends are never as troublesome to children as anxiety about their parent's welfare, especially if there is only one parent around and he is vulnerable.

Was father deserted? Does he feel women are untrustworthy? Or that he is inadequate in some way or other, unable to have held on to his wife? These events built into the family system affect the child's development and comfort with male and female roles and relationships.

Families with one parent are similar to those with two parents. Who is inside the family, the cast of characters, is less important than the system and the process, the script itself. With a parent who has a good self-image, a good feeling about herself and her sex, a desire and ability to relate to the opposite sex in a family which can show care and concern, good controls, and clear communication with the children, the system will be vulnerable but balanced and functional. The children will grow up able and anxious to relate in a two-parent partnership later on. What is inside the mother (or father) and how it affects the family system and its functioning, her capacity for flexible, adaptive response to her extra challenge, is even more important than the history of events that made and kept it a one-parent family.

BLENDED-FAMILY SYSTEM

BLENDED FAMILIES consist of family parts that come together as new families. There are children who live with two adults, only one of whom is their natural or original parent, and the family includes in very important ways the other parent, even if he is dead or divorced and living elsewhere. The tasks of this kind of group, in addition to the usual ones, include (1) negotiation of roles and boundaries (who does what and who means what for whom?), and (2) making room for all the members. Husband and wife have some previous experience in family living, which can be of great value, yet they may also have a heightened sense of vulnerability, a reluctance to trust new relationships because of difficulties in the past and the breakdown of the original family and the aftermath.

These families must learn to live with "ghosts" from the past, some emotional conflict or trauma surrounding the loss of the parent who is now gone. Such residual problems, when combined with the tasks of daily living in a dynamic, changing family of growing children, can make family life a difficult challenge. More than this, the rule of sticking together and standing by each other —the commitment that is the basic rule for all families—has been broken at least once in the past.

The tasks of blended families are complex, and members must learn to deal with change—moving, new people, and changing circumstances—more than in a nuclear family. Feelings and wishes which may interfere with efficiency in adaptation are pushed aside. The power structure of the family and authority issues (who's boss; how and why?) are the crucial areas of negotiation. New living patterns, including authority, cannot be dictated. Moreover, there usually has been an intermediate structure of a one-parent family in which rules and discipline might have been lax or overly strict and arbitrary. If mother now insists to her children, "He's your new father. You listen to him," children will rebel or submit with a feeling of helplessness. If mother had no authority in the old one-parent family, children do not listen to her in the first place. They will ignore both adults, detach from the family wherever possible, and relate only when forced to obey. A prospective spouse who hears "These children need a father" may well suspect that he is being invited into a trap. The children *have* a father, and the new stepparent is a stranger. If the new spouse does not respect the original family structure and does not relate to the children through the mother and the natural father, he will be like a dictator without followers, or alternatively, like a helpless ruler over chaos. Relatives and grandparents who knew about, or perhaps even contributed to, difficulties in the first marriage also will have judgments and agendas of their own which must be worked through over time.

In visitations, different parent figures start out all having authority over the children, yet parents who do not live together and perhaps are angry or competitive with each other communicate little with their former spouses. Emotionally involved, usually through anger, yet unwilling to speak to each other, they use the children to "deliver the message" or "light the fuse" for one another.

Arbitrary decision making and a battle for power, each parent undercutting the other when the other is absent, are frequent patterns. Two sets of parents and two, three, or four sets of grandparents, each arguing or refusing to speak to the others, can insist that the child do things their way, and their way only. Children learn to manipulate and end up with more power than either parent, usually feeling depressed about it because they perceive it as the loss of their parents. Parents without authority are no parents at all. The adults in these kinds of situations use the child to deal with their own feelings of resentment, jealousy, or curiosity toward the other adults. Children have mixed loyalties and rebel against orders received from preoccupied grownups who require that they become the enemy of one parent and a spy for the other, alternating allegiances with weekends.

The blended family is based on a contract different from that of the first marriage. While sexual difficulties or emotional dissatisfaction are the biggest problems in first marriages, money and children—the concrete evidence of former family existence—are the problems in second marriages. One or both individuals have a sense of failure or loss from a previous marriage, perhaps a problem with separation from the original family of origin, a loyalty conflict that may have made the first marriage itself vulnerable. However, parents of a newly married couple, even if they are not autonomous, are at least separate. Now, instead of in-laws, there are children who "come first" or are one spouse's own "private burden," skewing the relationship, preventing the balance out of which a good partnership and "differentiation" grow. Roles and capacities have not grown out of a common history coherently over time. There are fixed expectations that each member has of the others, a part that each actor is expected to play. There is little communication about these roles before marriage because needs are usually great, hopes are high, and expression of feelings and wishes is dangerous. The fantasies of the spouses and the premarital courtship bliss vanish just as they do in first marriages, but this time the children are blamed. Mother cannot control their feelings about the new stranger, and conflict and disappointment become a threat to the fragile continuity of the family. It is important for these families to understand that the more comfortable and open children feel and the more they express their anger and confusion, the better it is for the family. Breakdown of phony complacency and expression of hostile feelings can be a sign of progress, the first step toward new negotiation.

The roles and tasks vary with the individual involved. For the children, questions include, "Who is this man? What should I call him?" After a history of change, possibly disruptive, traumatic, dreaded, change in the home as it was, there is a feeling of powerlessness, a sensitivity to anything that might be arbitrary in the structure or rules of the new household. There is a resentment and a fear of intrusion, an awakened yearning and sympathy for the natural father. Children must learn to trust the new stranger by working with him over time.

A new stepfather (or stepmother) should know the needs and expectations he has of his new family. Does he have a need to be loved and accepted or respected and obeyed by the children? His best course is to put aside such expectations, accept his status as a stranger, work with the children on a daily basis, not requiring any commitment from them. Obedience is not allegiance and allegiance is not love. Love is a product of intimacy, not a requirement for it. A new stepfather must above all respect the relationships that the child has with both natural parents, especially his rival, the natural father. He must know that the child's own self-respect is linked to the image he has of his father. A dead parent should not be idealized, nor should his memory be denied or blocked out.

For the mother, there can be a conflict between loyalty to her children and a desire to please a new spouse. She should be aware of the origin and limitations of her expectations regarding her spouse and children, respect the loyalties and relationships of each individual family member, and negotiate changes in authority and power structure of the family slowly. Children must also work out the new relationship with their natural father, as well as any ideas they may have about whether one parent was hurt in the original family, and their tendency to identify with that parent.

Over the course of time, as trust increases and communication opens up, members will talk about the disappointments so that new contracts can be negotiated—variations on the original fantasies but based on realistic possibilities. New people will fill old roles in their own way. When the adults can accept their place in the family superstructure and can communicate with the children and with each other, accepting everyone else's past, real family living can begin. Former spouses can realize that you don't have to love or even forgive someone in order to communicate with him; you just need to accept his separateness and his humanity. Communication is more than words; it implies an awareness and an expression of feelings, as well as taking responsibility for one's own wishes and thoughts. Children can then be open and can communicate confusion, the first step toward working out loyalty conflicts, without worrying about overburdening or alienating various adults. They let the grownups settle questions that require adult responsibility, no longer fear moving out of the family field for school and other activities, and resume living their own lives in an emotionally meaningful way. As mentioned earlier, there is in all families a constant swing in the life cycle between attachment and detachment, intimacy and autonomy, security and freedom. The special challenges that many non-nuclear families face can inform all of us about these universal aspects of the human condition and of the family.

XIV

——— ∽ ———

GOVERNMENT,
THE FAMILY,
AND THE FUTURE

E̲ARLIER, IN CONSIDERING prevention, the focus was on the emotional environment, individual growth, and expectations over the course of time in the family field. It is crucial to include society and its arm, the government, in our thinking about these issues. Forces from outside shape us just as powerfully as forces from inside, and these forces, such as government and "experts," depend upon feedback from all of us concerning how we are affected, and how successful and reasonable our changing societal structure is becoming. Feedback to legislators is especially important because solutions abound during times of dissatisfaction and crisis. And in the social sciences especially, they can often create new problems requiring new solutions. They confuse issues further and induce a feeling of helplessness in those tackling complex problems.

Most of these "solutions" encompassing new styles of marriage and child rearing start as social experiments but end by touching upon issues of law and government: family law, domestic relations, social programming, welfare, health-care funding, and research. Government is increasingly expected to perform functions previously belonging to the family—economic, educational, and recreational among them. Recently, more basic functions involving nurture, child care and "child's rights" have been discussed by governmental agencies. Are such functions quantifiable, manageable by administrators, and can they be performed by people who are interchangeable, relieving parents of parenting?

In most human affairs, but especially in child rearing, it is impossible to separate who performs a function from the function itself. Even in giving economic support, the government must understand aspects of family systems; otherwise, welfare and funding programs have unintended effects, such as undermining families while simultaneously discouraging autonomy of individuals. (Families of tremendous wealth and welfare families handle money the way their family structures dictate. Some are oblivious and some are overly concerned.) The way we divide supplies and spend money is crucial to governmental decisions about mechanics and amounts of financial support.

Governmental interest in education has focused on earlier and earlier stages of development, encouraging a return to the family for that function as well. Head Start programs work best, if at all, when parents are involved. Dr. Burton White tells us that educational competence seems to depend upon attitudes of the mothering figure, a kind of availability without intrusion, and the physical structure of the family, especially rules about exploring and wandering in the first three years of life.

But more than any of these functions, emotional growth and well-being cannot be supplied like a vitamin outside the context of a continuous human relationship. There can be great variation in what parents do in their interactions with their children, but the message that one is valued as a human being, the identification with older family members, being nurtured and controlled and learning to nurture and control and value oneself, require a stable personal structure that allows time to assimilate such ideas. The environment where one is valued and protected according to one's needs, where some (the adults) have more power than others (the children), where differentiation between the sexes is considered to be the norm, where these ideas can be *felt*, then known in the context of various one-to-one relationships, is not one that can be delivered by the state.

Professor Barbara Finkelstein has documented the history of the government's involvement in child care. Laws concerning children have usually been something of an afterthought, piggy-backed to appropriations that provided money for wars against the Indians, the Civil War, and foreign wars. When they felt that families were not caring for children adequately, legislators tended to recommend separation of children from their parents. This occurred most specifically with Indian families in the nineteenth century and later with black, urban, and immigrant families in the cities. The Children's Bureau was a governmental organization that was established in 1912 and operated on the assumption that the health and welfare of children were directly related at all times to the capability of their family to provide care for them. This agency was dissolved in 1968.

What has happened since then? In 1974, Title 20 of the Social Security Act combined Aid to Dependent Children and Child Welfare in the original Social Security Act, and this is an example of how we encourage separation of children from other family members. When financial support is conditional upon job retraining, legislators probably think they are encouraging independence and autonomy, whereas they are really dictating the terms for survival. They are "saving the children" as they did American Indian children a century ago. Parents get the message that they will receive public assistance when there are children in the home whom they must leave. These families are supposed to become, as if by magic, middle-class families. If parents received financial support when they cared for their children themselves, it would mean that the government valued parenthood, and the feeling of solidarity in these vulnerable families would be enhanced.

There are few fields in which well-intentioned recommendations can have paradoxical, unexpected effects like the social sciences. For instance, punishing mothers for child abuse can increase the abuse. The mechanism is easy to understand. Mothers who punish their children because they feel guilty punish them more when they are made to feel guiltier. Big government, especially enlightened big government, can be excellent government. But governments do one thing, families do another. The benevolent intrusion of experts and administrators of social services can and has undermined the structure of families because paradoxical, counter-intuitive feedback mechanisms were not understood and because various hidden agendas, unarticulated but powerful, were being satisfied. Aid to Dependent Children, through which financial support was provided to families without fathers, is an example of the former. Housing subsidies that were aimed toward improving ghetto conditions without addressing discrimination, isolation, and other important societal issues concerning families, are a good example of the latter.

Countervailing trends in our society are confusing because there is no common value system. For instance, the movement for self-actualization and freedom from the "constraints" of family life seems to be at odds with the "child's rights" movement. Systems thinking shows how this is not the case. Professionals work for a child's rights movement because of our failure in many cases to respect and care for our children properly. Now, however, in many cases we have the phenomenon mentioned earlier that Dr. Solnit describes as "abandoning children to their rights." There is a feedback relationship, not simple cause and effect between our feelings, our behavior, and our statements concerning our children. Parents are invited to abrogate their responsibilities when professionals and government seem to take them over. The reality is that children have rights, but they are inextricably tied up with the social and family system of which they are a part. There can be no child's rights without parents' rights and family rights. In fact, it is the old problem of communication—confusion between what is said and what is real. Throughout our history children's services like kindergarten, nursery school, and day care have in reality been *mothers'* services. Family services are children's services.

The child advocacy movement comes from our own identification with children and our discomfort with parenthood, our wish to be children rather than parents. Often we drown our children with our "caring," yet we are reluctant to be authoritative because it deprives them of "liberty." We confuse politics with child development, and society's functions with family functions.

One of the striking features of the government's policy is the myth that the government has no family policy. The government only taxes, spends money, and functions in hundreds of other specific capacities. Issues about the government and family policy engage Americans violently, and statements about the family can only get politicians into trouble. When Vice President Mondale was in the Senate he was a member of a Family Impact Seminar to determine the effects on families of legislation and other government activities, especially those of HEW. He probably knows as well as anyone in the Administration how "charged" this topic is.

What about this myth? First of all, the government dictates the terms for financial assistance for our citizens. If a family needs welfare, it is better if father does not remain in the home. Yet mother should be willing to identify who the father of any child is. Social Security does not recognize the contribution of homemakers and allows benefits in accordance with the number of households rather than the number of adults.

As an employer, the government sets up work schedules and affects the family lives of its employees. (It could experiment with "flex-time," dovetailing work and school schedules probably better than any other employer in the country.) Next, like other medical insurers, Medicare and Medicaid encourage institutionalization. In housing, the government promotes stratification of families by age, creating "age ghettos." It spends nine times as much money for foster care as it spends on homemaking services. Finally, it regulates the economy trying to control inflation and unemployment, sometimes giving us generous portions of both. Inflation short-changes people with a fixed income and the elderly, while unemployment brings increases in child abuse, suicide, homicide, and mental-hospital admissions.

NINE O'CLOCK, a busy time in the emergency room with four or five surgical and medical patients, yet there was more noise and more pain in the one consulting room than in any other area. No medical emergency, no surgical crisis. A boy had a black eye, yet there was chaos. A nurse, a police officer, a doctor, two aides, and a government researcher, a physician interested in child abuse, were all hovering around the family. Mark, thirty-seven, and his wife,

Cindy, were at opposite ends of the room. Mark had his head in his hands. He had been crying. Cindy was telling the police officer the story. In the next room the nurse treated Mark Junior's black eye with ice. Mark didn't want treatment. He wanted to go to his father. The nurse looked angrily into the other room at Mark Senior. She thought that her patient wanted to jump up and slug his father and she helped the two aides in restraining him. The police officer was saying, "Everybody settle down." Suzy, Mark's younger sister, was in the waiting room outside, distraught, picking her nails, biting her lip. Her younger brother, David, was at home, supposedly watching television.

This family was under severe tension. The professionals who had come to help and "put out the fire," which they had done very effectively two hours before, were now preventing a natural healing process. Mark Junior was worried about his father, who was severely depressed even before the incident. Mark Senior had lost his job a year earlier, had been staying around the house all day and all night, and had been drinking heavily the last few months. Mark Junior had provoked his father to get him off his mother's back, to get him to stop drinking, and to get *some* kind of response out of him, anything, and finally he had achieved his goal. He was completely unaware of his black eye. He wanted to forgive his father and stand by him and help him. The last thing he wanted was to get even or to get protection *from* his father. Suzy and David at home were in an acutely anxious state. The family needed to be together right away to resolve this crisis, and later perhaps, the members needed to learn how to get more distance from one another.

Suzy went home to get David, and the family met with a counselor in the emergency room to discuss the evening's events. Mother told the story again. Mark Junior had spoken up one time too many. He liked to butt in between his mother and his father. His father, with three beers under his belt, thought Mark Junior had not shown "proper respect," and he had hauled off and hit his son in the face. The counselor turned to Mark Senior and asked him about himself. He felt like a failure but he loved his family, including Mark Junior. Here was the irony of his family and every other one like it. It was his *love* for his family, his guilt over his failure to support them, that made him so irritable. Now his unemployment had run out. He had fixed everything there was to fix around the house in the first month. After that he was bored, irritable, and began drinking. He gave up looking for work after six months. His prospects were minimal. The family could move, but a move would disrupt school for the children. Besides, they had no place to go. He would have to "wait it out," for the economy to pick up.

The counselor wondered about other ways in which Mark Senior did not feel like a man, what the sexual relationship between husband and wife was like, whether he was increasingly jealous and suspicious of his wife despite the fact that he spent the entire day at home. The counselor had found just these kinds of problems in the epidemic of troubled families he was dealing with during the current recession.

He recommended things for the family to do that their father could direct: visits, trips, things that would be important to the family, and he recommended a follow-up visit with mother and father and a willingness to "wait it out" with them all until Mark got his job back.

This case is typical of thousands across the country that occur in epidemic proportions when unemployment increases. They occur most frequently in industrial areas and affect middle-class families more than others.

In every family the people who have the problems and the particular problems they have will vary with how successful family members feel and how flexible they can be with their view of themselves.

HOW CAN the government do its work and help us and our families? First of all, it cannot solve all of our problems. But it can recognize and monitor, in a continuous way, the effects on families of legislation, court decisions, and fiscal and monetary policies of any kind, not just those of HEW.

There might be a Family Bureau rather than a Children's Bureau, government support for Community Family Life Centers like the two in Maryland, which could deliver health-care services as well. As a nation, the United States leads in medical technology but lags far behind other industrial countries in disease prevention and health-care delivery. Clearly, the reason for this poor performance is the government's endorsement of an outdated moral code that realizes individualism but fails to acknowledge the importance of each person's family and milieu. The day-care issue provides a good example not only of the confusion between family and societal functions, but also of the results of our outmoded mystifying morality.

Day care helps us solve a number of real problems while simultaneously allowing room for some of our favorite fantasies. It lets middle-class mothers do the most important thing one can do in our society—that is, go to work. Women can be similar to, superior to, and together with men while day care keeps their children safe, educates them, and feeds and cares for them uniformly (as their parents try to make more money than their neighbors). It also gives, according to our fantasies, lower-class children from educationally deprived family backgrounds an opportunity to "catch up." Upper-class children, on the other hand, go to "nursery schools" and "play groups."

"Day care." The word is intriguing. Does it mean what it says? Care during the day? It usually refers to group baby-sitting, and the educational, therapeutic, and rehabilitative work with the children is frequently only in our fantasies. It does allow mothers, however, to be free of "day caring" for their children. One wonders if the word, a lovely word in itself, will someday bring problematic and unpleasant associations like two other formerly lovely words, "welfare" and "Willowbrook."

The case against day care is a strong one. First of all, what do we mean by "care"? Care implies attachment. Dr. E. James Anthony quotes Dr. Mary Ainsworth: "Attachment is 'an affectional tie that one person forms to another, binding them together in space and enduring over time.' It involves primarily positive feelings toward the other person, it is confined to a few people, takes time to develop and is obviously a factor in the survival of the individual and of the species."

We know that children need a constant mothering figure, a continuous relationship early in life to develop a sense of trust and a belief in a predictable reality. Work schedules, vacations, and job changes so prevalent in the social science and caretaking fields (one out of three social workers changes jobs every year) do not fit well with children's emotional needs. It is difficult, in other words, to structure these aspects of the mothering function in labor-market terms.

The evidence from Sweden, Hungary, Russia, and Israel is not comforting. Young adults raised on the kibbutz want to raise their own children when they become parents. Many think that on the kibbutz, children are too peer-related, dull, and lack creativity, and attribute these characteristics to their communal upbringing. Russian child-care specialists increasingly emphasize the importance of the family. In Hungary they now pay women to stay home and raise their own children. People who work in the day-care system there almost never send their own children to a center. Dr. Spock, for one, is against day care.

It takes many years for professionals to study the effects of day care on children's emotional development. The evidence is not in, in our own country, and in those with more experience the trend is away from day care.

Cost estimates in the United States range from a modest $450 million per year (Representative John Brademas' House bill estimate) to a more rounded $33 billion per year (the cost for *quality* day care in the United States for lower-income families using existing real costs in New York City).

Perhaps family day care, paying mothers to raise their own children at a very young age while baby-sitting for other older children, is one possible solution.

The cases, however, for and against day care miss the point. Day care is here to stay, a necessity for our increasingly heterogeneous society. Women are joining the work force in ever-increasing numbers. And anyone who doubts that a good day-care system is unnatural or unfeasible should learn about the day-care system in the People's Republic of China.

But the solution to the problem does not lie in the method or the design of the day-care center. The solution lies within ourselves and our families, because the problems with day care come from our misconceptions, our ambivalence toward our families and our children, our confusion about the value of parenting.

This explains one of the many complexities about day care: the more "underprivileged" a child is, emotionally not economically, the less capable he is of being on his own even for a few hours and getting something out of a day-care center.

Yet those who want day care for their family should have guidelines on what these centers should provide and how they should be structured. There *are* environments that encourage growth, and it *is* possible for children in day-care centers to grow and develop normally. Some children even in institutions grow up without the emotional shallowness and poor intellectual development that institutionalization *can* produce. To some extent we can extract principles of environments which are healthy for our youngsters. According to Dr. Bettye M. Caldwell, children need a place where they can be safe, yet as unrestricted as possible. There must be organization to the environment, a sense of structure, a schedule for doing different things in order for children to develop a sense of predictability about the world around them. There must be materials for play. But more important than the things themselves, there must be adults around who give the toys and objects some meaning and value. Ideally, there should be frequent contact with adults of both sexes, adults who *like* children, who can show their caring and still set limits, without destructive criticism of the child's attempts at mastery. We need adults who can share tasks, as in China, where children begin *working* at tasks which *matter* to the school and the family at the age of three. We need adults who can give but not impose a sense of their own morals, preferences, and feelings, offering a value system which will not become a liability for the child later on. We need men and women who take satisfaction in the child's own development, tolerant not only of the child's dependency but of his growing autonomy. Dr. Caldwell can predict I.Q. at age three better if she knows about a child's environment and the interactions he has with adults than if she knows the performance of the child himself on tests of mental development at six, twelve, or twenty-four months of age. Most important of all, just as caring adults imbue objects with value for the young child, families imbue other adults in schools and day-care centers with a sense of value and acceptance for the children.

If we were clear about the line between the family and society, especially as regards family and government functions, if we were comfortable with ourselves, if we believed in the value of our families, were tolerant of those who wish to have and raise children, as well as those who choose not to, day care would cease to be a political football and we would have day-care centers worthy of our children. If we loved our children, we would be willing to keep them or part with them, depending upon the needs of the family. My reservation about day care concerns children in the first few years of life. Those parents and families who decide to have children should accept a caretaking role during the child's infancy, just as women accept the physical togetherness of pregnancy. As a society we can help such families feel respectable in every way possible, especially as regards work schedules, leaves of absence, and services both formal and informal for mothers and fathers of infants.

The return of a meaningful value system and the recognition of the importance of the family go hand in hand. The family is the crucible for values in a society, and a clear definition of what we want to do with our lives, based on such a value system, helps the government to respond to our needs promptly and effectively. The Carnegie Council on Children recommends that we tailor our work schedules to our family needs, increasing our availability during times of crisis and change. In Sweden there is an allowance for *paternity* as well as maternity leave without penalty, financial or otherwise. The Carnegie Council also recommends a guaranteed family income to replace other forms of financial support. Professor Urie Bronfenbrenner points out that the United States is the only modern industrial nation without health insurance or minimum income for families with children. We need such supports and we need them without the degrading, counterproductive relabeling process that is required when a family enters the welfare system. There should be family involvement in day-care centers and schools, all institutions where family-related services are performed. Financial policies, not only of the government and the welfare system but of the private sector—for instance, concerning living arrangements and even airline fares—should promote cohesion in families. There are many other ways of improving our lives through our families. Our commitment as individuals to plan and maintain our communities and their services depends largely on how we support and contain our families. We must always remember that we construct our societies, as well as our families.

But we can only be comfortable by knowing *ourselves, through* our families, guarding the families that nourish us by working on our societal structures. The facts about child development and periods of vulnerability should be respected. Day care can wait until children are two or three years of age. Those people who undertake to have children should know that divorce is hard on children under five years of age. Divorce as an immediate necessity, as the "solution" to all of one's problems, is usually a fantasy. The same fantasy exists about marriage. Despite our "Literature of Reassurance," divorce for a family with children is seldom "creative" and more often disastrous, and it should be dealt with as such. It is an unfortunate fact of life for many families, but individuals should know that they can take steps to minimize the damage to family members.

It is time to acknowledge the different functions of the family, especially as regards child rearing. Making babies requires more than making love. Not all married people need children or ought to have them. There are many different kinds of marriages, and over the course of a man's lifetime, or a woman's even longer lifetime, many kinds of liaisons are possible. When people do have children, they should accept the responsibility that raising children entails, and they should have respect for parenthood in our laws and in our rhetoric. Parents are the ones who deliver "child's rights" and no other way is currently feasible. Those who create children are the best ones to "save" them. We must be acutely aware of the effects on families of any social or governmental policies, administrative, educational, or financial. Currently the system is such that we spend the least amount of money for children who are at home with the family. We spend more to maintain a child in a foster home than in his own home, and the most money to institutionalize him. According to Professor David Fanshel of Columbia University, it costs five times as much to maintain a child in an institution as it does to keep him at home. Obviously, mothers could be subsidized for staying at home raising their children, since they usually work in the first place only to bring in more money for the family. Respect for the family during one's childhood, and reflected in society as a whole, is as important as information from courses and learning experiences later on.

Many of the common enemies that we faced together as a nation with a common value system have been overcome. Pollution, discrimination, poverty and anomie, however, are still with us. And with enlightenment and spiritual strength, we can endure. As time passes, there will be new challenges and new adjustments, new areas of growth and change for the family. What is crucial is that each of us realize that the family is our most important asset, whatever form it may take. The family as an institution is different from, but necessary for, society; it is not about to be replaced. As long as there are men and women who beget children, adults with authority, and children with a future, birth, growth, decline, and death, there will be families as we know them.

GUIDE TO
LEADING FAMILY
THERAPISTS

LEADING SCHOOLS of family therapy research and training have continued to refine and expand their techniques. In the poll taken for the GAP report mentioned earlier, the therapists cited according to their influence on family therapy around the country were Virginia Satir, Nathan Ackerman, Don Jackson, Jay Haley, and Murray Bowen. In a later study by Dr. Vincent Foley of St. John's University, the author of an excellent recent textbook on the subject, family therapists selected at random chose the same five individuals in a slightly different order as being the most influential. In a more recent meeting of the American Psychiatric Association, Drs. Murray Bowen and Salvadore Minuchin presented their most recent theoretical formulations, and Minuchin would surely be added to an updated list.

Virginia Satir, the most influential family therapist, according to these polls, works by helping people get in touch with themselves and their feelings. She helps them accept *all* their feelings, and to recognize a whole range of possibilities in themselves and in their intimate relationships. She focuses on the communication between family members and how it might be improved. A communications specialist, a virtuoso recognizing and dealing with feelings using a wide range of verbal and nonverbal techniques, she travels widely and her work is perhaps the best known of any family therapist in or out of the field of psychiatry.

Murray Bowen has developed perhaps the most definitive theoretical framework. He focuses on helping people to "differentiate," to develop a more secure sense of the self, more control and awareness in their psychological functioning, and more autonomy, all by understanding their family systems, especially their origins in families of the past. His work and Satir's were discussed in Chapter 3, "Exercises in Understanding Your Family."

Ivan Bosyormenyi-Nagy and Geraldine Spark understand families in terms of loyalties, bonds that transcend generations and geographical boundaries, and determine the value system, purpose, and emotional matrix. Nagy and James Framo edited the first major textbook in the field, *Intensive Family Therapy,* in 1966.

Dr. Nagy's work is known widely in the United States and Europe, and deals with the ethical implications of family therapy and human relationships.

James Framo, like Bowen, also works with the roots of current problems, life styles, and relationships in the families of the past, and works frequently with families of origin directly in his sessions. He frequently asks, for instance, the parent of a child or adolescent with a problem to bring in his (or her) own parents (the teenager's grandparents), and the adolescent patient usually settles down more quickly than with any other approach. Framo goes masterfully from understanding the individual's experience to the difficult decision about whether to change the system or to respect it and leave it alone. This is one of the most difficult technical problems for family therapists, especially beginners in the field. Framo also works effectively with marital couples in groups.

Gerald Zuk has expanded his concept of therapist as "go-between" who takes over this role from a family "go-between." He takes control of the family and establishes some new rules through which family members can resolve old disputes. Zuk, Nagy, and Spark were at Eastern Pennsylvania Psychiatric Institute (EPPI); the other "team" in Philadelphia, Minuchin and Jay Haley, is at the Philadelphia Child Guidance Clinic.

Salvadore Minuchin began his work with poor, fragmented families at the Wiltwyck School in New York. He learned to use nonverbal maneuvers, rearranging seating, changing the cast of characters, and focused directly on goals without necessarily exploring the inner emotional experience of members, or why a particular reaction occurred. His structural view of the family was presented in Chapter 5, "The Family as Life-Support System."

Jay Haley was originally at the Mental Research Institute in Palo Alto and formulated some of the earliest and most important work in the systems approach to family therapy. His focus is on problem solving, observable phenomena, and communication patterns, the rules and power structures that they imply, and how change comes about. (Often it is the result of a power struggle between the therapist and the family.)

While Haley is now in Philadelphia, John Weakland, Paul Watzlawick, and Richard Fish carry on at the Mental Research Institute in Palo Alto, continuing to focus on how people in families change. Among other things, they currently work with families on a short-term basis, usually ten sessions or fewer, to produce changes of a specific desired type. They refrain from doing or saying anything family members have already heard from friends, therapists, or one another, and attempt to "re-frame" or change the context or frame-work around a particular undesirable behavior. Sometimes they do the opposite of what a family expects—for instance, "prescribing" a symptom or a problem only to see it disappear because now the problem exists in a different context (for the therapist, not for the purpose or person for whom it was originally created).

Norman Paul in Boston found that all too frequently families are unable to handle a particular crisis or problem because of unresolved feelings of grief over a loss, especially if it is felt by one family member in particular. Vulnerable families have a member with unresolved attachment to someone no longer present and available. Paul helps families mourn together, free themselves from the past, live in the present, and plan for the future together.

John Bell works with adolescents in a three-stage process, changing the need for adolescents to isolate themselves, shifting the family structure and rules so that young people can express themselves toward their parents without being forced to bury or act on their feelings outside the family. Initially he changes the rules for communication, with little concern for what the particular messages are, or how correct or justified they might be. Later he works toward using this new openness in the most constructive way for each family member. His pragmatism and his use of family-process concepts provide a good example of modern family therapy. He allies himself, sympathizes, and makes a "secret pact" with parents of a troubled or depressed adolescent—he makes them promise that they will let the youngster speak his mind without interruption and also acquiesce to certain demands. Almost immediately the whole atmosphere of the family begins to change. Everyone behaves in a new and different way, surprising the others. When the adolescent's emotional pressure diminishes, Bell guides the family members into mutual communication, and they soon do not need him at all. Depression and delinquency stop and communication starts.

In 1977 a number of workers, including Drs. Murray Bowen, Ivan Nagy, James Framo, and Gerald Berenson, founded the first national organization, the American Family Therapy Association. Family institutes around the country continue to flourish, not only "on both coasts and in Philadelphia" but all over the country. They provide treatment and training for family therapists, as well as a framework for them to meet formally and informally to exchange experiences. At Tavistock Clinic, psychoanalysts like Henry Dicks developed special expertise on treating disturbed marriages. Family therapists trained in the United States now function in England, Mexico, Scandinavia, Italy, Israel, and Greece.

There is in the name of family therapy an enduring change in health care for all, the sick and the well. The changed approach is a synthesis of the "whole patient" concept of psychosomatic medicine of the 1950s with systems theory, and deals with the social context of human beings, their physical and emotional welfare, and their emotional growth.

Under the diversity of theories and styles, which seem to vary with the times and with the particular talents and training of the family therapists, there is on a deep level a congruence between the different schools. Therapists work in a framework of psychotherapy. People come to a presumed "expert" with a problem or a goal, and he helps them work toward a solution. The goals for all family therapists are those of health or growth or change. If one views family therapy as a conceptual framework, a family approach to handling the problems and tasks of living, family therapists probably exist and function in every society where there are families.

FAMILY THERAPY CENTERS

THE FOLLOWING is a list (by no means complete) of family therapy centers where treatment and training are available. I apologize to the many excellent and dedicated family thrapists who have worked in this field over the years but who are not mentioned here.

EAST

Boston Family Institute
  1170 Commonwealth Avenue
  Boston, Massachusetts 02134
Cambridge Family Institute
  144 A. Mt. Auburn Street
  Cambridge, Massachusetts
   02138
The Creamery
  Shelbourne, Vermont
Waterbury State Hospital
  Family Therapy Service
  Waterbury, Vermont
Department of Psychiatry
  Yale University School
   of Medicine
  New Haven, Connecticut
Ackerman Family Institute
  149 East 78th Street
  New York, New York 10021

Albert Einstein College
  of Medicine
  Jacobi Hospital
  Eastchester Road &
   Morris Park Avenue
  Bronx, New York
Center For Family Learning
  10 Hanford Avenue
  New Rochelle, New York
   10805
Columbia College of Physicians
  & Surgeons
  Dept. of Psychiatry
  722 West 168th Street
  New York, New York
St. Luke's Hospital Center
  Dept. of Psychiatry
  Amsterdam Ave. & 113th Street
  New York, New York
Family Studies Section
  Bronx State Hospital
  1400 Waters Place
  Bronx, New York

Jewish Family Service of
  New York
  33 West 60th Street, eighth floor
  New York, New York 10023
Payne Whitney Psychiatric Clinic
  New York Hospital–Cornell
    Medical Center
  Family Therapy Dept.
  525 East 60th Street
  New York, New York
Dept. of Psychiatry
  University of Rochester
  Medical Center
  Rochester, New York
Westchester Family
    Consultation Center
  Green Ridge Avenue
  White Plains, New York
Family Institute of Philadelphia
  259 South 18th Street
  Philadelphia, Pennsylvania
    19103
Family Psychiatry Division
  Eastern Pennsylvania
    Psychiatric Institute
  Henry Avenue &
    Abbottsford Road
  Philadelphia, Pennsylvania
    19129
Family Therapy & Sex
    Therapy Sections
  Dept. of Mental Health Sciences
  Hahnemann Medical
    College & Hospital
  Philadelphia, Pennsylvania
    19102
Philadelphia Child
    Guidance Clinic
  Two Children's Center
  34th Street & Civic Center Blvd.
  Philadelphia, Pennsylvania
    19104

Georgetown Family Center
  4380 MacArthur Blvd, N.W.
  Washington D.C.
Center for the Study of
    Human Systems
  8604 Jones Mill Road
  Chevy Chase, Maryland 20015
Family Therapy Institute
  300 Connecticut Avenue
  Washington, D.C.
Groome Child Guidance Center
  5225 Loughboro Road N.W.
  Washington, D.C. 20016

SOUTH

Atlanta Psychiatric Center and
  Center for Personal Growth
  6363 Roswell Road
  Atlanta, Georgia 30328
Dept. of Psychology
  Georgia State University
  Atlanta, Georgia
Dept. of Psychiatry
  Medical College of Virginia
  Richmond, Virginia
Dept. of Psychiatry
  University of North Carolina
  School of Medicine
  Chapel Hill, North Carolina
Family Therapy Institute of
    Greater New Orleans
  Suite 505, 111 Rue Iberville
  New Orleans, Louisiana 70130
Community Guidance Center of
    Bexar County
  San Antonio, Texas
Timberlawn Foundation
  Dallas, Texas
Routh Center
  Dallas, Texas

Children's Mental Health Services
  of Houston
  Houston, Texas
TRIMS—Texas Research
  Institute of Mental Sciences
  Houston, Texas
University of Texas
  Medical Branch
  Dept., of Psychiatry
  Galveston, Texas
Methodist Home
  Child Guidance Center
  Waco, Texas

MIDWEST

Family Institute
  2600 Euclid Avenue
  Cincinnati, Ohio 45219
Family Institute of Chicago
  Ten East Huron
  Chicago, Illinois 60611
Family Study Center
  University of Missouri-
  Kansas City
  1020 East 63rd Street
  Kansas City, Missouri 64110
Dept. of Psychiatry
  Medical College of Wisconsin
  Milwaukee, Wisconsin
Menninger Foundation Family
  Therapy Training Program
  Topeka, Kansas 66601
Minnesota Family Study Center
  218 North Hall
  University of Minnesota
  St. Paul, Minnesota 55108
Dept. of Psychiatry
  Wayne State University
  Detroit, Michigan

Dept. of Psychiatry
  University of Wisconsin
  School of Medicine
  Madison, Wisconsin

WEST

Brigham Young University
  Dept. of Child Development
  and Family Relations
  Provo, Utah
Dept. of Psychiatry
  University of California
  Medical College at Davis
  Sacramento, California
Dept. of Psychiatry &
  Dept. of Clinical Psychology
  University of Colorado
  Medical Center
  Denver, Colorado
Depts. of Psychiatry & Psychology
  UCLA School of Medicine
  Los Angeles, California
Dept. of Psychiatry
  University of Washington
  School of Medicine
  Seattle, Washington
Family Therapy Institute
  of Marin
  1353 Lincoln Avenue
  San Rafael, California
Family Therapy Center
  3529 Sacramento Street
  San Francisco, California 94118
Mental Research Institute
  555 Middlefield Road
  Palo Alto, California 94301
Project
  2010 Hearst Avenue
  Berkeley, California 94709

CANADA

Institute of Community and
  Family Psychiatry
Jewish General Hospital
Montreal, Canada
Marriage and Family
  Treatment Center
University of British Columbia
Dept. of Psychiatry
Vancouver 8, B.C., Canada

EUROPE

The Tavistock Institute of
  Human Relations
School of Family Psychiatry
Tavistock Centre, Belsize Lane
London, N1V3, 5BA, England

Dr. Douglas Hooper
  Dept. of Mental Health
  University of Bristol
  41 St. Michael's Hill
  Bristol, BS2 8DZ, England
The Institute of Family Psychiatry
  Ipswich and East Suffolk
    Hospital
  Ipswich, England
Psychosomatische Klinik der
  Universität Heidelberg
  Monchhofstrasse, 15A
  Heidelberg 69, West Germany
Italian Society for the Study of
  Systems Communication-
  Family Therapy, Children,
  and Adolescents
  Centro Minerva Medica
  via Lazzaro Spallanzania
  9/11, Roma, Italy 00161
Centro per lo Studio della
  Famiglia e delle
  Techniche di Gruppo
  via Leopardi, 19
  Milano, Italy 20123

ABOUT THE AUTHOR

HARVEY WHITE, M.D., is a psychiatrist and family therapist in private practice in New York City. Currently, he is also Director of the Family Crisis Unit at St. Luke's Hospital in New York, as well as an assistant clinical professor in the Department of Psychology at Columbia College of Physicians and Surgeons. One of the founding members of the American Family Therapy Association, Dr. White has written several articles on family process. He is on the staff of Hackensack Hospital and affiliated with St. Clare's Hospital in New Jersey. Dr. White lives with his family in New York City.